ADHD
RAISING AN EXPLOSIVE CHILD

THE 7 SKILLS OF POSITIVE PARENTING TO EMPOWER KIDS WITH ADHD. LEARN HERE THE EMOTIONAL CONTROL STRATEGIES TO HELP YOUR CHILDREN SELF REGULATE AND THRIVE.

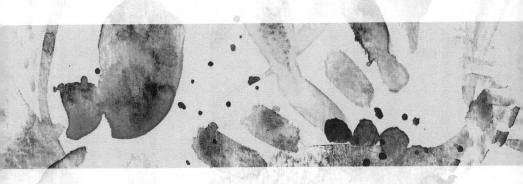

JOANNA BRAIN

TABLE OF CONTENTS

INTRODUCTION

What is ADHD?

Attention-deficit Hyperactivity Disorder (ADHD) is one of the most common mental disorders affecting children. ADHD additionally impacts lots of adults. Signs of ADHD consist of inattentiveness (not having the ability to keep focused), hyperactivity (unusually or abnormally active), and impulsivity (rash acts that occur in the minute without thought).

An approximated 8.4 percent of children and also 2.5 percent of adults have ADHD. ADHD is usually initially diagnosed in school-aged children when it brings about disruption in the class or troubles with schoolwork. It can, likewise, impact adults. It is more common among boys than girls.

What Does It Mean to Have ADHD?

Has anybody ever asked you if you have ADHD? Possibly, you've also wondered yourself. The only way to understand for sure is to see a physician. That's because the disorder has a variety of possible symptoms and they can easily be confused with those of other conditions, like clinical depression or stress and anxiety.

Not sure whether a doctor should assess you? If a number of these apply, you may need to see a doctor.

1. People say you're absent-minded.

Everyone loses cars and truck keys or jackets from time to time. This happens when you have ADHD. You may hang around looking for glasses, wallets, phones, as well as various other products each day. You may also forget to return calls, space out on paying bills or miss medical consultations.

2. People complain that you do not pay attention to.

Most of us lose concentration on a discussion from time to time, specifically, if there's a TV nearby or something else demanding our interest. It takes place typically and also more

frequently with ADHD, even when there are no diversions around. Still, ADHD is even more than that.

3. You're typically behind schedule.

Time management is an ongoing challenge when you have ADHD It usually results in missed due dates or appointments unless you deal with preventing that.

4. You have difficulty concentrating.

Issues with interest, mainly focusing for extended periods or taking notice of details, is just one of the characteristics of the problem. Depression, anxiousness, and also addiction problems can likewise take a toll on your ability to focus, as well as many individuals with ADHD have one or more of these problems, too. Your doctor can ask your questions to get to the root of what's causing your attention issues.

5. You leave things undone.

Problems with interest and also memory can be challenging to start or complete developments. Specifically, ones that you know will take a lot of attention to finish. This symptom can indicate depression, as well.

6. You had behavior concerns as a child.

You need to have had attention as well as focus troubles as a child to be identified with ADHD as an adult–even if those early signs didn't feature an official diagnosis.

Individuals might have accused you of laziness back in youth. Or they may have thought you had an additional problem like depression or stress and anxiety.

If you were diagnosed with the disorder as a child, you might still have it. The signs change as you age, and also not everybody outgrows it.

7. You lack impulse control.

It is more than tossing a sweet bar right into your cart at the checkout line. It is doing something even though you understand it could have severe repercussions, like running a red light because you believe you can get away with it or otherwise being able to keep the peace when you have something to state, even though you recognize you should.

8. You cannot get organized.

You might discover this more at work. You could have difficulty setting goals, following up

on tasks, and meeting project deadlines.

9. You're nervous.

Children with ADHD are typically hyper, but adults are more likely to be fidgety or troubled. You might also talk too much, as well as to interrupt others.

10. You can't control your emotions.

You may be irritable or short-tempered, express frustration usually, feel indifferent or be susceptible to angry outbursts. ADHD can make it tough to handle awkward feelings or follow ideal habits when you're disturbed.

The Various Types Of ADHD

Comprehending ADHD

Attention deficit disorder (ADHD) is a chronic condition. It primarily influences children, but can additionally impact adults. It can affect emotions, behaviors, and also the ability to learn.

ADHD is divided into three different types:

1. Inattentive type

2. Hyperactive-impulsive type

3. Combination of both types

Signs and symptoms will determine which sort of ADHD you have. To be identified with ADHD, signs, and symptoms have to influence your daily life.

Signs and symptoms can alter over time, so the type of ADHD you have might change as well. ADHD can be a long-lasting obstacle. Medicine and various other therapies can help improve your quality of life.

Three Types of Symptoms

Each sort of ADHD is tied to several qualities. ADHD is identified by inattentiveness and hyperactive-impulsive actions.

These Behaviors Are Frequently Present in All Types:

Inattentiveness: being sidetracked, having the inadequate concentration and also organizational abilities

Impulsivity: disturbing, risk-taking

Hyperactivity: never appearing to slow down,

talking as well as fidgeting, problems remaining on task

Everyone is different, so it's usual for two individuals to experience the very same signs in different ways. For example, these behaviors are typically mixed in young boys and also girls. Children may be seen as more hyperactive, as well as girls may be silently unobserving.

Inattentive ADHD

If you have this type of ADHD, you may experience a lot more signs and symptoms of inattention than those of impulsivity as well as hyperactivity. You might battle with impulse control or hyperactivity at times. These aren't the primary attributes of inattentive ADHD.

People who experience inattentiveness commonly:

- Miss details and also are sidetracked quickly

- Get tired rapidly

- Have difficulty concentrating on a solitary task

- Have trouble organizing thoughts and also

learning brand-new info

- Lose pencils, papers, or various other things needed to finish a task

- **Don't appear to pay attention**

- Move slowly and also look as if they're daydreaming

- Refine details much more slowly as well as much less appropriate than others

- Have a problem following directions

More women are detected with inattentive type ADHD than children.

Hyperactive-Impulsive ADHD

This type of ADHD is defined by signs of impulsivity and attention deficit disorder. People with this type can present indications of inattentiveness. However, it's not as significant as the various other symptoms.

People that are impulsive or hyperactive frequently:

- Squirm, fidget, or feel restless

- Have difficulty sitting still

- Talk continuously

- Touch as well as play with objects, even when inappropriate to the task at hand

- Have trouble engaging in quiet tasks

- Are regularly "on the move"

- Are impatient

- Act out of turn and also don't think of repercussions of actions

- Spout out answers and also inappropriate remarks

Children with hyperactive-impulsive type ADHD can be an interruption in the classroom. They can make discovery more challenging on their own and even other students.

Combination ADHD

If you have the mix type, it indicates that your signs and symptoms do not exclusively fall within the inattentive or hyperactive-impulsive behavior. Instead, a mix of signs and symptoms from both of the categories is displayed.

Many people, with or without ADHD, experience some level of unobserving or spontaneous behavior. Yet it's extra dangerous in individuals with ADHD. The behaviors frequently occur as well as interferes with just how you function at home, school, work, and also in social circumstances.

The Central Institute of Mental Health clarifies that many children have combination type ADHD. The most common symptom in preschool-age children is hyperactivity.

Causes Of ADHD

The reason for ADHD in your child can be traced back to family members. The condition is genetically based, which in simple terms, implies your child may have been predisposed due to your genetics. Even though conditions in your home or school can add to it, they do not consider ADHD reasons.

There have been lots of scientific analyses that link physical attributes to the source of ADHD. These include genetic makeup, absorbing toxic active ingredients, trauma to the brain, and responses to some artificial additive.

The Make-Up of Your Genetics:

Check out other members of your household. Did you recognize that even though three to five percent of children are identified with ADHD, 25 percent of an ADHD child's relatives will certainly additionally have the condition? Scientific researchers have also disclosed specific genes that have been linked to the root cause of ADHD!

Toxic Components:

If you consumed alcohol or made use of tobacco products while you were expecting, and also you have an ADHD child, researches have indicated a possible link. A fetus will certainly absorb these poisonous compounds, which certainly cannot be excellent. If your child has been around old buildings, he may have been revealed to lead poisoning. Several of these toxic ingredients have been labeled as possible ADHD causes. When I was growing up on a farm, my Dad subjected me to DDT, which is currently outlawed in the USA. Possibly, that added to my ADHD, and then my boy's.

Brain Injury:

Most children, fortunately, don't come under this category; however, specific sorts of mental trauma can bring on ADHD signs. Scientific studies had shown that when an ADHD child and a non-ADHD child had brain scans or an MRI, there were some distinctions in some regions of the mind. This would seem to show that the brain has something to do with the source of ADHD.

Food Additives:

About 10 percent of ADHD children show minimized signs when their sugar and additive intake has been reduced. Currently, right here is somewhat of a shock. While a lot of us, including me, tend to associate sugar with attention deficit disorder, there was no difference when children were given either sugar or a sugar replacement. That suggests that sugar doesn't contribute to ADHD signs.

Given that a lot of individuals have it in their heads that sugar triggers ADHD symptoms, they may see more signs after a child has some sugar. Studies reveal that moms and

dads that believe that their children have been provided sugar (when they have been offered a substitute) are just as most likely to state that ADHD signs have worsened as parents of children that are given actual sugar.

Even if it is only considered, a reduction in sugar consumption (or high fructose) can be beneficial.

A recent study has discovered that preservatives and also food coloring, which can be found in soft drinks as well as fast food, significantly increase hyperactivity in children. So, make sure you see what they are taking into their bodies.

Remember, ADHD triggers children to act in unacceptable means. However, it doesn't need to be this approach. It is an extremely treatable problem. There are prescription drugs that work for the signs, natural remedies that attack the origin of the condition, nutritional control, and behavioral therapy. Do your study, and after that, do what is in your child's best interest.

CHAPTER - 1

IDENTIFYING SYMPTOMS

ADHD Symptoms at Every Age

Symptoms on their own do not suffice to make an ADHD diagnosis, but they are key warning signs to help identify the problem and treatment for your child. In general, childhood ADHD signs are a hyperactive, reckless, and impulsive behavior combination. The diagnosis is usually made if the symptoms occur in at least two different settings over six months. Yet did you know that the symptoms of ADHD tend to change with age? Here are some basic suggestions for deciding if your child needs a doctor and an ADHD assessment.

ADHD can be found in pre-school years. However, the difficulty of the diagnosis is that children in this age group are usually hyperactive and inattentive. ADHD symptoms become a little more apparent when children

start school and need to be present in a structured environment. They may not be able to follow simple directions, sit down or wait for their turn. They could talk, move, and jump from one activity to another constantly. Please note that several developmental disabilities also share these symptoms, so make sure the doctor of your child performs a thorough evaluation rather than just reviewing the list of symptoms.

During the primary school years, the symptoms of ADHD in the school environment become even more evident. In the middle of discussions, children with combined type ADHD and hyperactive ADHD tend to get up from their seats, talk over, or blur answers. Those with an inattentive ADHD form are much harder to detect. They are typically well-pleased kids of mediocre grades, often because of trouble completing their homework or following instructions. They spend more time dreaming in class than paying attention and avoiding tasks that require a lasting focus. They could also be the messiest children in the classroom.

During the high school years, ADHD can

easily remain undetected in all schools; if the child is clever enough, they can make up for their symptoms. Nonetheless, secondary education poses a serious challenge to children diagnosed with ADHD due to heavy workload and greater obligations. Schoolwork is not only a problem, but ADHD is often associated with other problems such as low self-esteem, eating disorders, and dangerous behaviors such as drug experimentation and casual sex. Since the difference between the usual mood swings of teenagers and ADHD symptoms is difficult for the parents, get professional help if you see major mood, socialization, and school performance changes.

ADHD Symptoms in Children

Attention Deficit Disorder Hyperactivity In children:

Some studies show that the top ten factors of ADHD sleep disorders are why some people can't sleep at night. Many individuals with ADHD sleep disturbances remain awake in bed two to three hours until they sleep. Stress is not being able to sleep easily can cause other forms of psychological and physiological imbalance

that lead to depression and other forms of mental problems in the sufferer.

The bad thing is that many parents hesitate to seek help with ADHD for their children because they can blame themselves for causing this type of behavioral problem. But understand, it's no one's fault because inside of the brain lies the problem. Please seek treatment immediately if you suspect your child has ADHD.

Reports have shown that about one percent of children with ADHD symptoms are treated. If untreated, ADHD can ruin your child's future. He or she is likely to drop out of school, cannot make friends, and cannot keep jobs. Don't let your child be a victim of that. ADHD children can easily be identified from regular healthy children. Children with ADHD have symptoms such as being unable to remain focused, not being able to remain calm, not staying in a seat, and often having problems with their behavior, causing problems in school and at home.

The treatment for ADHD usually includes stimulants. When children with ADHD are treated with stimulants, they can make better choices, are not repulsive, do not take to risky

behaviors. They are less likely to be violent than children who are not cared for.

In addition to treatment, interventions such as short-term goals, a lot of reinforcement and consistent boundaries and consequences will help the child to learn how to control their behavior.

ADHD Symptoms and Your Child's Education

There is no relief from the fact that it can be quite a difficult task to teach a child who has ADHD symptoms, who brings all the' baggage' usually brought by the underlying ADHD diagnosis. These difficulties are often seen to be the worst when finding a school that is suitable for any child with such ADHD symptoms.

Many schools know this, as well as the difficulties faced by children suffering from ADHD (and other types of attention deficit disorder–ADD). These more illuminated schools have often already recognized the problem by taking major steps to address it.

Nevertheless, most schools are still behind, and often they are not in a position to meet the needs of a child with ADHD symptoms

and characteristics. Sadly, even before any formal evaluation of the illness of the child is undertaken, the often-negative effect of a child affected by ADHD can often clearly be seen in the classroom.

It may be seen, for example, in the annoying boy who is continuously distracting his friends, or in the little girl sitting in the corner playing with her hair and her mind somewhere else.

It's usually not surprising that the teacher recognizes first that there are problems in a particular student or that they are unnecessarily overactive. Nonetheless, defining the condition is only the first move and definitely not the hardest part.

This will, no doubt, be the result of altering the subconscious or hyperactive actions of the infant, and it is obviously unrealistic for anybody to expect the signs of ADHD just to go away!

Of course, before any type of 'treatment' process can begin, everyone must recognize and agree that the disorder exists. It is only after such a correct diagnosis that appropriate action can be taken.

At this point, the decision will then have to be taken as to whether or not medicinal products are needed.

The critical decision is the often-invasive nature of many chemical drugs, and the extent of the ADHD symptoms shown by the particular child would normally be determined. This will also determine the course of the following therapy, perhaps for the long-term, and it is, therefore, essential to arrive at the correct conclusion.

Now that ADHD is accepted as a condition that tends to be unpleasant to others, some schools can take the easy way out of it by giving the child sometimes unnecessary medicines.

Nevertheless, other schools will take a more patient approach and avoid drugs wherever possible, generally in line with the child's parents ' wishes. If you have a child with ADHD symptoms at school, then your child may be coping with the situation depending on the type of school they are in.

In the ideal world, your child should be in a school that understands that everyone can work together as a team in the most effective way to

deal with ADHD problems. You need to accept and understand that the ADHD symptoms of your child won't just' go away.' Only through the recognition and dealing with your child's ADHD (or sometimes around it) can a school allow your child to do their best.

Unfortunately, however, many schools lack this open-mindedness and vision, particularly in small communities or in those where money can be scarce. No question that it is difficult and even harder to instruct a child with ADHD symptoms because they are often quite chaotic and disruptive characters. It's therefore perhaps no surprise, but no less disappointing, that even nowadays some schools are refusing to accommodate such disruptive children.

On the other hand, a growing number of schools accept and support children affected by ADHD, making significant efforts to help them.

Sometimes this is done by placing the child with the disorder in corrective classes, even though a school thinks that this' differentiation' of a child can lead to isolationist problems for the long term.

Another school is set up to handle the child with all the other children who have ADHD symptoms in the' normal' class. Where this works, it is certainly the most successful round solution, but for this to be achieved, often scarce resources must be allocated, thus making it out of the financial reach of many institutions.

Recall that your child cannot help in the final analysis to show and demonstrate the symptoms of ADHD, and cannot always control the actions and behaviors that result from their condition.

As a parent, it's your job to accept your child as they are and to always look after their well-being. Therefore, you should always make sure that you discuss with your child's teachers all matters concerning your child to reach a conclusion that is in the best interests of your child.

Remember, they did not choose to exhibit and act the effects of ADHD symptoms accordingly.

Identifying ADHD Symptoms for Proper Treatment

Naughty, obedient, and spectacular–these are only a few words used to describe people who have impulsivity, indifference, and hyperactivity. To the untrained eye, these are only bad behaviors. But is it valid, has to be more of what you see?

Attention deficit hyperactivity disease is a condition that can be hyperactive, impulsive, and inattentive for both children and adults. This is a developmental disorder, usually before a child turns seven, and when not controlled, it can persist into adulthood. Understanding various ADHD signs is of the highest importance for the proper treatment of attention deficit hyperactivity disorder. It helps you to see if you or one of your loved ones has ADHD.

These are split into three for a better understanding of the specific ADHD symptoms in children. The first is for inattentive signs and symptoms that occur when the child makes several careless errors, is distracted, and has difficulty keeping focused. The child also pays no attention to details and when you talk to

them, they seem not to listen. There will also be trouble following directions, and they have problems arranging and preparing their things in advance. In the case of the signs of hyperactive ADHD, the child is constantly fidgeting, is unable to hold still, walks quickly, talks loudly, has a short temper, and is restless. Impulsive signs of ADHD are seen when the child does not care when they cannot wait for their turn during plays when they are on track when they speak, they disrupt others, and they cannot control emotions.

Adults with hyperactivity disorder with attention deficit have symptoms of ADHD different from those of children. One of the most common ADHD symptoms seen in adults is difficulty focusing. They are easily distracted, they still fail to complete their tasks even worldly, their listening capacity is weak, and often miss specifics. For some people, they will be hyper-focused or will tend to become too absorbed in rewarding things.

CHAPTER - 2

THE CAUSATIVE FACTORS OF ADHD

ADHD is a highly heritable disease, but in addition to genetic causes, often inherited and environmental influences that may be prone to prevention or alternative treatment are discovered. The causes of ADHD can be classified as idiopathic, naturally arising from an unknown cause, symptomatic, and secondary to a structural abnormality of the brain, or from family and assumed genetics. Most ADHD cases are idiopathic or cause uncertainty. A delay in nervous system development or maturation is often suggested as an explanation for ADHD, particularly for children with moderate or "soft" neurological deficits.

Etiological Classification

Sometimes, the etiologies of ADHD are defined by the time they occur:

(1) Prenatal;

(2) Perinatal; and

(3) Postnatal.

The syndrome may be inherited and family, or acquired and environmentally friendly. Rarely, the root cause of ADHD is a chromosomal disorder.

Prenatal factors include neurological developmental deficiency, maternal anemia, pregnancy toxemia, drug and cocaine misuse, and smoke from tobacco. Many environmental factors that are often suspected include exposure to arsenic, water and diet PCBs and pesticides, lack of iodine, and hypothyroidism. The birth season may be a risk factor, and exposure to viral infections, especially influenza and viral exanthema, has been associated with ADHD diagnosis in the first trimester of pregnancy or at the time of birth.

Perinatal etiological causes include premature birth, breech delivery, anoxic-encephalopathy, hemorrhage of the cerebrum, meningitis, and encephalitis.

Postnatally the child may have had a head injury, meningitis, encephalitis, repeated otitis

media attacks, or low blood sugar. Drugs used in the treatment of childhood disorders, asthma, and epilepsy, often induce or intensify hyperactive behavior and result in delays in attention and learning. Diet's role in causing ADHD is uncertain, but the ingestion of food additives and saccharose, lack of omega-3 fatty acids, and allergies to certain foods are sometimes important. Potential causes and occasionally, thyroid hormone deficiency are associated with ADHD are known as lack of iron in the diet and anemia (Millichap, 2008). An abnormality of sensory feedback soothed by oral potassium is suggested in a 9-year-old boy with symptoms of sensory overstimulation and potassium sensitivity as a novel cause of ADHD.

Evidence for a Neurological Basis for ADHD

The neurological or anatomical theory of hyperactivity and ADHD are focused on various animal laboratory trials, neurological and electroencephalographic (EEG) experiments, and brain magnetic resonance imaging (MRIs). Studies of positron emission tomography (PET), revealing improvements in the glucose

metabolism in the brain's frontal lobes, point to a localized cerebral abnormality in adults who have been hyperactive since childhood.

Neurological "soft" symptoms are characteristic of right-sided frontal cortical lesions, including motor persistence (incapacity to maintain postures or movements), distractibility (incapacity to maintain attention), and careful control and reaction inhibition. The largest number and degree of hyperactive behavioral responses derive from frontal cerebral lesions and their associations with the basal ganglia or striate cortex. The right prefrontal cortex plays a part in regulating attention and inhibiting responses, while the basal ganglia are involved in motor regulation and behavioral responses. In children with ADHD, distractibility and impulsivity represent deficits in response inhibition.

Injury or irregular development in regions of the brain other than the frontal lobes can also be associated with ADHD syndrome and language and social competencies deficiency. For children with temporal lobe lesions, cognitive dysfunction and ADHD are identified,

and in such cases, a link with the front striatal circuitry is likely.

In 4 children with bilateral medial temporal lobe (hippocampus) sclerosis, associated with severe epilepsy, starting in early childhood, deficits of cognitive function, language growth, and social skills were identified at Duke University Medical Center, Durham, NC. MRI displayed irregular signals and hippocampal volume loss of 25 percent.

In some patients of childhood, the temporal lobe arachnoid cyst is identified in combination with ADHD. The diagnosis of this relationship and condition, though rare, points to the possible significance of prenatal factors in the cause of ADHD. The cause of arachnoid cyst is typically undetermined, but trauma, bleeding, or virus infection is likely to cause damage to the fetal brain. In patients with elevated intracranial pressure and complicated headaches or seizures, care may include surgery to remove the cyst, but other, more restrictive interventions may usually control the symptoms.

Analyzes of brain volume by MRI. Measurements of different brain structures using quantitative

MRI techniques have revealed changes in corpus callosum size, decreased volume of right prefrontal cortex and basal ganglia, smaller cerebellar vermis, and smaller cerebral volume. In children with ADHD, MRI measurements of the right prefrontal cortex and basal ganglia correlate with response inhibition and task success. Decreased cerebral volumes can explain lower scores on IQ tests in some children with ADHD.

At the Western Psychiatric Institute, University of Pittsburgh, PA, the MRI volumetric study revealed differences between task performance and prefrontal and caudate volume in the right hemisphere in 26 children with ADHD as opposed to 26 normal controls. Only the right prefrontal measures correlated with inhibition-including response efficiency.

In the ADHD group, quantitative MRI studies in 46 right-handed boys with ADHD and 47 matched healthy controls at the National Institute of Mental Health, Bethesda, MD, found a smaller cerebellar vermis, especially involving subsequent inferior lobules. Within ADHD, a malfunction of the cerebello-thalamo-

prefrontal circuit is postulated.

Localized cerebral hemisphere and cerebellar developmental abnormalities in ADHD are associated with an impaired striatal-cerebellar frontal activity, and often with a stimulant response.

At the University of California, Irvine, volumetric MRI brain analysis showed smaller volumes of localized hemispheric structures in 15 male ADHD infants, compared to 15 normal controls. Smaller left basal ganglia (specifically caudate nucleus) was associated with stimulant drug response while non-responders had reversed caudate asymmetry.

MRI tests of the head of the caudate nucleus at the University of Barcelona, Spain, associated with neuropsychological disorders and behavioral problems in 11 adolescents with ADHD. The ADHD group had a larger right caudate nucleus, and the usual L > R caudate asymmetry had been reversed.

The multiple anatomical sites of brain damage or lesion that are often found in children with ADHD that account for the syndrome's varying

symptoms and complications.

Based on cerebral blood flow, EEG tests and volumetric MRI measurements, a frontal-motor cortex disconnection syndrome, or "lazy" frontal lobe, is proposed in ADHD. This idea is derived from the frontal lobe's role as an excessive motor activity regulator, with children with ADHD having disinhibited motor activity. Methylphenidate's calming effect may be attributed to a relaxing effect on the frontal lobe inducing motor inhibition.

EEG ADHD and Anomalies. For children with ADHD with varying frequencies, epileptiform discharges in the EEG are recorded from 6% to 53%. The reason for an EEG in ADHD includes:

(1) A history of seizures;

(2) Repeated "daydreaming;"

(3) A history of brain trauma, encephalitis, or meningitis; and

(4) A reference to stimulant therapy in patients with an epileptic background or family history.

(5) A proportion of ADHD patients are more vulnerable to seizures, based on EEG evidence.

Computerized power spectral analysis for EEG statistical analysis reveals that boys aged 9–12 with ADHD have increased theta (4.75 Hz) and decreased beta 1 (12.75–21 Hz) activity relative to age-and grade-level controls (Mann, 1992). The increased theta is located in the frontal and central locations, and in posterior and temporal areas, the beta decreased.

EEG results from 184 boys with a combined form of ADHD showed three distinct EEG clusters or subtypes of children distinguished by

Increased slow-wave activity and rapid wave deficiencies;

Increased theta of high amplitude with beta deficiencies; and

An excess beta community.

As far as the EEG profile, kids with ADHD don't comprise a homogenous class. Quantitative EEG information in kids with ADHD may give more precise proportions of mindful issues than are presently accessible from abstract polls or rating scales. Inconstancy of EEG attributes must be recollected whether soon the EEG is utilized as a dependable analytic technique for

ADHD.

Impact of Genetic Factors in Etiology of ADHD

Families would also admit that during infancy, fathers and mothers were hyperactive or had a learning problem. They will also dispute any childhood behavior or attention issues, despite being unable to sit quietly during the consultation. It's not unusual to have a history of relatives and cousins diagnosed with ADHD who have had a positive reaction to stimulant medication.

It is hard to prove the strong difference between the influence of nature and diet in the cause of ADHD, and both the genetic and acquired factors are significant. The cause may be solely genetic in some cases, in others, primarily acquired and environmental, and in others, a mixture of both. Epidemiologists use many methods to demonstrate the function of genetic factors as opposed to environmental influences.

(1) ADHD predominance in various geographic, ethnic, or racial populaces.

In an investigation of 145 kids determined to have ADHD at the Shaare Zedek Medical Center, Jerusalem, Israel, young men dwarfed young ladies by 3:1, 30 percent had kin with learning inabilities contrasted with only 7 percent among control kids without ADHD, and 34 percent were of North African root, an ethnic gathering present in only 12 percent of the number of inhabitants in Jerusalem. A familial-hereditary factor right now patients were reflected by the dominance of guys, the expanded pervasiveness of learning troubles in kin, and an ethnic-related inclination to ADHD.

(2) Risk of ADHD in first-degree family members (guardians, kin, and offspring) of patients with ADHD contrasted with everyone:

Of the 457 first degree family members of youngsters and teenagers alluded to the Child Psychiatry Program, Massachusetts General Hospital, Boston, the danger of ADD, just as introverted and temperament issue was generously higher than among regular controls.

(3) Twin investigations: One may liken indistinguishable, monozygous (MZ) twins with brotherly, dizygous (DZ) twins. IF hereditary

elements are noteworthy, both MZ twins are influenced (concordant), while for common kin, concordance in DZ twins is lower, and indistinguishable. For ADHD inquire about, DZ twins must be of a similar sex, because there is a male prevalence. A case of the job of natural impacts in the advancement of ADHD is how much MZ twins might be conflicting (i.e., just one influenced).

An assessment of 10 sets of twins, at any rate, one of which had the hyperactive condition, found that every one of the four sets of MZ twins was dependable, while just one of six sets of DZ were concordant. The twins at the MZ were all young men. A hereditary reason for ADHD is affirmed by this exploration.

The Minnesota Twin Family Report, including 576 twin young men matured 11 and 12, and educator and maternal examination survey, confirmed the job of hereditary factors in the treatment of ADHD subtypes of both obliviousness and hyperactivity-hastiness. Natural conditions had less etiological supporters of ADHD.

Twin studies using ADHD interview testing at the UCLA School of Medicine, Los Angeles,

CA, revealed 79 percent concordance in 37 monozygotic twins, compared to 32 percent in 37 same-sex dizygotic twins. ADHD is a genetic disease with a prevalence of five to six times higher in the first-degree genetic compared to the general population. ADHD proband relatives have increased levels of comorbid conditions, especially oppositional and behavioral disorders, anxiety, mood disorders, and learning disabilities. Studies of adoption endorse both a genetic basis for ADHD as well as environmental causes.

CHAPTER - 3

ASSOCIATED CONDITIONS OF ADHD

As if a diagnosis of ADHD is not enough for a parent to worry about, there are often other conditions that develop in conjunction with ADHD or simply as a reaction to ADHD. Children with ADHD and an associated condition require that much more time, attention, and medical care. It is believed that approximately half of all people with ADHD also have another condition. In children, the Centers for Disease Control and Prevention estimates that approximately 2/3 of ADHD children have another disorder. Associated conditions can be mild or severe. They might be directly linked to ADHD, or they might be a condition that has simply taken its time to show up and announce its presence. These additional conditions fall within two categories: secondary conditions and comorbid conditions.

Secondary conditions are those that are a direct result of the ADHD. When a child is dealing with ADHD, it can be quite a frustrating and stressful situation for him. In many cases, other conditions develop because they are triggered by frustration and stress. As treatment of the ADHD progresses, these secondary conditions often become more manageable or fade away entirely. Comorbid conditions are conditions that exist concurrently with ADHD. They are not going away with the ADHD treatment. In fact, comorbid conditions usually need their own specific treatment program. You and your child's doctor must determine which additional conditions are secondary or comorbid.

The number of associated conditions a child or adult can have along with ADHD is basically endless. There simply is not enough time or book space to discuss every possible medical condition because they are not all definitively associated with ADHD. However, it is important to know some of the common conditions and their possible symptoms because when it comes to ADHD, knowledge is power. While not an all-inclusive list of probably related conditions, the following list describes many of

the more prevalent associated conditions.

Anxiety

We have all felt a little anxious at some point in our lives. Anxiety manifests itself as feelings of stress, worry, being tense, being tired, and several other symptoms. However, the fleeting anxiety the average person feels is not considered a disorder. Chronic anxiety affects about 30% of ADHD children and approximately 50% of ADHD adults. These feelings of worry and stress can have a detrimental effect on the quality of life. Depending on whether or not the anxiety begins to diminish with ADHD treatment determines if it is a secondary or comorbid condition.

Depression

Depression is a mood disorder that affects almost 15% of ADHD children and almost 50% of ADHD adults. Only about 1% of non-ADHD children suffer from depression. Depression is more than a few moments of feeling sad. Everyone feels sad from time to time. Depression is a serious disorder that involves feeling unhappy, moody, irritable, and even worthless. These feelings

do not go away. Depression affects more than just your mood—it reduces your interest in life. It requires treatment, often including therapy. Depression may occur because of ADHD or because of environmental factors and genetic predisposition. In most cases, it is considered a comorbid condition.

Learning and Language Disabilities

As many as 50% of ADHD children have a type of learning disorder. When compared to only 5% of non-ADHD children having learning disorders, this number is quite compelling. Dyslexia and dyscalculia are two of the more common learning syndromes that may affect an ADHD child. Dyslexia has an impact on the child's ability to read and write. Dyscalculia impacts the child's ability to understand and perform math skills. Language disorders affect approximately 12% of ADHD children, while these speech problems only affect about 3% of non-ADHD children. Both learning and language disabilities fall into the category of comorbid conditions. They each require their own treatment plan.

Gross and fine motor skill difficulties

Fine motor skills include tasks like grasping a pencil with your fingers and writing. Gross motor skills include physical activities, such as jumping and running. Both types of skills require the use of certain small or large sets of muscles. ADHD can affect the fine and gross motor skills of your child. For example, you may notice that your child struggles to write neatly because his hand and fingers jerk around. Your child may seem awkward and overly clumsy, such as falling frequently or struggling to do a jumping jack, because the ADHD is affecting larger sets of muscles. These disorders are comorbid conditions and require their own treatment plan.

Obsessive-Compulsive Disorder

The obsessive-compulsive disorder, also known as OCD, may have you thinking of the hoarding shows on television. While hoarding certainly is a symptom of OCD, it is not the only symptom. This disorder can be mild or extreme. It can manifest itself in the form of repetitive behavior, like counting to a certain number while performing a task, or even pulling out hair.

49

OCD can also involve the extreme need to be clean, such as washing hands repeatedly, even until they are raw. OCD may involve hoarding, which is the overwhelming desire to collect certain items, or it can be a form of extreme anxiety to the point of being overly cautious. OCD is also a comorbid condition. Therapeutic treatment can be helpful, along with possible medications.

Oppositional Defiant Disorder

The oppositional defiant disorder is a common disorder associated with ADHD and known as ODD. This disorder results in extreme bouts of anger and/or rage. This is not a typical temper tantrum. ODD is an uncontrollable anger/rage that occurs during a meltdown that results from even the smallest trigger. These meltdowns can last just a few minutes or even as long as half an hour. When an ODD child has a meltdown, once he has calmed down, he is usually quite remorseful about what happened. This disorder can be secondary or comorbid. There are various types of treatment available.

Bipolar Disorder

Bipolar disorder is another mood disorder that has various symptoms. It is a comorbid disorder, so you cannot expect the ADHD treatment to fix the bipolar problem. Bipolar disorder often includes severe and unexplainable mood swings. For example, your child may be ecstatic and extremely happy for several days, only to suddenly switch gears to anger and rage that also lasts for several days. People with bipolar disorder have a hard time relaxing and calming down, especially when they are in a "manic" state of mind. There are numerous medical treatments to help control bipolar disorder because even though the "highs" feel great to the patient, the "lows" may feel worse than anything they have ever felt—possibly driving them to the point of suicide.

Tic Disorder

A tic disorder involves the physical twitching of certain groups of muscles. These muscles are often found in the face, neck, and shoulder areas of the body. You may notice short, jerking movements of your child's head that he cannot stop or control. You may even detect tics of

the eyes or the mouth, such as the rapid and uncontrolled blinking of the eyes or a chronic twitch at the corner of the mouth. Tics are most often noticed in children, and many children ultimately grow out of the tic disorder as they become an adult. It was once believed that certain stimulant ADHD medications caused tic disorders. However, more has been learned about these types of conditions, including the fact that there is a genetic factor to consider. It is now believed that the stimulant medications did not cause the tic disorder, the medication simply flipped on the internal, genetic predisposition switch residing within the child. Tic disorders are comorbid disorders and can be managed with appropriate treatment.

Tourette Syndrome

This is a syndrome that most people misunderstand. A person hears the word Tourette and they automatically assume that the afflicted will randomly blurt out swear words. This is not a movie—this is real life. It is also interesting to note that about 60-80% of people with this particular syndrome also have ADHD, but not even 10% of ADHD people have

Tourette syndrome. Tourette syndrome does vocally manifest itself. Think of it like tics, only it is tics of the vocal cords. People with this disorder may make odd noises randomly or repeat phrases indiscriminately, including the occasional swear word. However, uncontrolled swearing is not a realistic description of Tourette syndrome. This is a comorbid condition that requires a different treatment plan than ADHD.

Sleep Disorder

It is extremely common for ADHD children to have struggled with sleep. They may have trouble falling asleep, they may have difficulty staying asleep, or they may have both problems. Sleeping disorders are often a secondary condition of ADHD. There are treatments available that can help your child to fall asleep and stay asleep. These treatments used in conjunction with the ADHD treatment plan should make for a happier, well-rested child.

Abuse of Substances

Studies have indicated that ADHD children have a higher risk of smoking cigarettes at an early age. They also have an added risk

of following this nicotine dependence with alcohol abuse and, in severe cases, even drug abuse. ADHD children are twice as likely to develop an addiction to nicotine. It is important to note that studies show ADHD children treated with stimulant medications are less likely than their non-ADHD peers to abuse illegal stimulants, such as cocaine and methamphetamine. This may be a result of the opposite effect that stimulants have on ADHD children. These substance abuse problems are a secondary result of ADHD. In many cases, with the appropriate treatment, parents can be proactive and prevent substance abuse from ever becoming a problem by actively treating the ADHD.

Secondary and comorbid conditions include many more than this list defines. Your child could be suffering from any sort of condition at this very moment without your knowledge. That is why parents must be involved in their children's lives and keep the lines of communication open. Many of these associated conditions are serious and require their own form of treatment. If your child is diagnosed with ADHD, you cannot assume that the ADHD treatment plan is going

to solve all of the problems, both behavioral and emotional. Instead, monitor your child and his reaction to the treatment plan. If you still notice obvious problems, even after tweaking the treatment plan, it may be time to consider the idea that your child has an associated condition.

Obviously, this list of potentially associated conditions are quite overwhelming and it is not an all-inclusive list. Numerous other conditions are not mentioned, which could be associated with ADHD. Parents must keep in mind that an ADHD diagnosis does not automatically equate a diagnosis of a second disorder. It is also important to note that some of these associated conditions can be mistaken for ADHD. This is why a medical examination, testing, and professional diagnosis are necessary. If you treat your child for ADHD when he is actually suffering from bipolar disorder or anxiety and depression, it can pose a serious threat to his overall health and well-being. Associated conditions are not necessarily the norm— millions of children and adults cope with only ADHD daily. However, knowing about the possible associated conditions and recognizing

some of the symptoms helps to ensure that your child's mental health is always at its best.

CHAPTER - 4

ACCEPTING YOUR CHILD'S ADHD

It's one thing to be informed about ADHD and to learn all you can to better help your child. But actually, coping with an ADHD child daily can be very stressful and frustrating. It may be more so for you if you are the primary caregiver, but never forget that the stress can take its toll on your family as well. That's why the first thing you need to do is establish strategies to help you and your family cope and accept the situation.

Moving Forward

Learning that your child has ADHD triggers a rollercoaster of emotions; fear, grief, worry, anger and guilt, and shock. Your first question is going to be, how am I going to cope? How is my family going to cope? Take time to get over your initial shock and grief, but after that, it's time to get down to business.

The first thing that you and your family must do is accept the fact that the situation will not go away overnight–or anytime soon, for that matter. Your day to day life needs to more or less be structured around your child and everyone must do their part. Parents, grandparents, siblings and other immediate family members must all be patient and supportive until your child overcomes this challenging phase of his life.

How to Cope Emotionally as a Parent

Let's be honest. Discovering that your child has ADHD is extremely traumatic. You may have suspected it. You may have guessed that the symptoms and behavior your child gas been displaying were signs that he has ADHD. Nevertheless, the official diagnosis from the doctor is always a shock.

Acceptance is the only way you can move forward and start helping your child. This is easier said than done and it will be a very difficult time for you. Sincere acceptance of your child's condition is an important part of your emotional healing as a parent.

The following are the best ways you can overcome the emotional struggle and find peace in acceptance.

1. Allow yourself to mourn. As parents, we all have bright visions of what our children will be: well-behaved, high achievers at school, popular with friends, and praised by teachers. This vision is harshly shattered when a child is diagnosed with ADHD. Realizing that he will never behave like other children break your heart. Give yourself time to grieve and don't bury your emotions. It's okay to cry and feel sad. Acknowledging these feelings is the only way to release them.

2. Stop rejecting who your child is. Your first thoughts will probably be angry ones: Why can't my child be like everyone else? Why does it have to be him? What have I done to deserve this? What has my child done to deserve this? Acknowledge those thoughts, but don't believe them. Instead, challenge the thoughts.

3. Ask yourself the following question: Do you love your child any less because he has ADHD? Do you blame him for having ADHD? On the contrary, you probably love him even more

and want to do everything in your power to protect and shelter him. You love your child no matter who he is. This is another step towards acceptance.

4. See your child's positive strengths and be grateful that he is healthy and strong. ADHD does not disqualify a child from being gifted and talented in many areas. In fact, kids with ADHD are extremely talented and creative due to their natural exuberance and energy. Focus on these strengths and let then become your source of pride and joy.

5. Don't feel guilty. Guilt is usually the first reaction of a parent when they learn that their child has a disease or disorder. Your first reaction will be that you are somehow responsible, and this is normal. The only advice I can give you here is short and blunt. You are not responsible. It's not your fault. It's normal to feel guilty. Get over it!

6. Stop when you catch yourself fighting reality. Rejecting reality is a lost battle. This is when you find yourself hoping against hope that your child will suddenly start behaving differently or that his symptoms will suddenly go away. You

may even reject the fact that he has ADHD at all, thinking it was a misdiagnosis, and rush to get a second and a third opinion.

Ignoring the facts is emotionally damaging because a child with ADHD will not outgrow it overnight, and will never behave in the way you expect him to. When you catch yourself having these thoughts, stop immediately, and ground yourself in reality. Your child needs your help and support, not your wishful thinking.

The goal of all of this is to change your perspective so that you can emotionally process and accept your child's condition. Only then will you be able to move forward and be strong for yourself and the rest of your family.

Now that you are on the way to acceptance, it's time to incorporate more practical coping strategies.

1. Manage your stress. Stress is the number one struggle you will face when raising a child with ADHD. It is something you will face daily. Unless you have techniques in place to help you lower your stress, the effects on your physical and mental health can be very serious.

Take time out for yourself every day to wind down and relax. Meditate, practice yoga, exercise, take a quiet walk, or a warm bath. Practice a hobby or have a quiet lunch out with friends while your child is at school; whatever helps you to relax needs to be practiced regularly to avoid burnout. This is not a luxury but a necessity, even more so if you are juggling a busy career with a hectic family life.

Managing stress will also help you be more tolerant and calmer when dealing with your child and less prone to anger or frustration. The more drama you can avoid, the better for you and your child.

2. Join a support group. Encouragement and support from parents in the same situation are crucial. Search for these groups online or on social media platforms—you will actually be surprised to discover how many there are. This is a wonderful way to share your problems and concerns, exchange advice and exchange tips, advice and experiences with other parents.

If the group is local, you can even arrange to meet regularly and introduce your children to each other. Many support groups also arrange

lectures by experts to stay on top of the latest information on ADHD. They also arrange activities and outings for families. Knowing you are not alone and that your problems are common to many other people will help keep your resolve strong.

Helping Your Child Cope

The first thing you need to do is tell your child the truth. Do not wait for him to learn that he has ADHD from a teacher or classmate or by overhearing a conversation. First of all, he will think it more serious than it is and that you are hiding something terrible from him.

Second, your child may lose trust in you. It is your responsibility to be the first to inform your child about his condition and to explain the facts. A simple explanation in simple words is sufficient for very young children.

When your child is old enough to understand, explain to him the following:

Tell your child that he has a problem called ADHD

Explain the symptoms in simple terms, telling him that he will have difficulty sitting still, waiting for his turn or focusing for a long time, and that he has to work harder than other kids to be able to do that.

Explain that all children are different and have different needs. For example, some children like to sit still and do quiet activities while others, like himself, have more energy and have to move around more. Or, that while some children have to sit at the front of the class to hear and see well, he may need to listen more carefully to understand what the teacher is explaining.

Explain what ADHD IS NOT. For example, it's not being lazy or stupid or badly-behaved and hat, it's not something to be ashamed of. This is very important because sadly, these things may be said to your child by other people.

If your child is taking medication, explain that it will help him focus better. You can discuss other children you may know that are taking medication, such as for asthma, so that your child is reassured that medication is not a bad thing.

Get the point across that all people have things they are better at than others. Discuss your child's strengths, such as being able to draw well, run fast, be funny, etc.

Keep your explanation simple and explain only the basics.

Give your child honest answers to any questions he may have. The first question he will ask is, "When am I going to get better?" Do not raise the child's expectations. Tell him that both of you have to work hard together and he will start to get better slowly, but that it will take some time.

Discuss the strategies you will follow together to help him deal with ADHD.

Tips for Helping Your Family Cope

If you have other children, the first thing you need to do is explain to them that their sibling has ADHD. Simplifying as needed depending on their ages. Explain that all of you must work together to help their sibling, as he may not always be able to behave in the same way that they do.

Let them know that you expect them to help their brother or sister whenever they can and to never, ever taunt him about his condition. Never hesitate to enforce strict discipline when this is done.

The following strategies should be followed by the whole family. Lead by example and your other children will learn to behave and interact in the same with their sibling.

Celebrate the "pros" of ADHD. Children with ADHD often have special gifts that can be supported and encouraged. Creativity, spontaneity, energy, and enthusiasm are some examples. Point out these gifts to your child often.

Help your child whenever appropriate. For example, when he is really struggling with a certain task. Encourage your family to help with homework and engage in therapy whenever possible.

Structure family and household rules and activities that will allow your child to succeed. For example, giving him shorter chores to accomplish, making a list of things he needs to

do so that he can cross each one-off. Structure and schedule playtime with siblings where he can engage in the games he likes.

Monitor playtimes if possible so that the child does not get over-excited. Be on the alert for fights breaking out between siblings or other children and intervene at once.

When assigning larger tasks, enlist a sibling to help your child succeed in complete them.

CHAPTER - 5

PARENTING A CHILD WITH ADHD

CHILDREN WITH ADHD often need extra care and attention from parents, teachers, daycare workers, and other caretakers in their lives. Young children who are hyperactive need more careful monitoring to make sure they don't get themselves into situations where they might get hurt. An older child might need some extra attention and effort to keep busy and actively engaged in things that interest her or him. A child in elementary school or middle school might need some extra help in getting organized and keeping track of things, making sure assignments get turned in, and coordinating efforts between teachers and parents.

To which my question is—so what? It is almost comical how many books written for parents of children with ADHD start with the message that "parenting a child with ADHD is so very

hard, you poor parents deserve a medal!" To which I say: hogwash. Also, pure unadulterated nonsense. Whoever said parenting was supposed to be simple and easy? Beyond that, let's not put these children into a different category of children. They're just children.

Maintaining a healthy perspective is important. The child with ADHD did not "catch" ADHD out of pure thin air. Statistically, there is a very strong probability that one or both parents, or one or more grandparents, also have ADHD (sometimes it skips generations, depending on the genetic load). If ADHD biology is part of your family's genetic history, the most constructive way to deal with it is to accept it, understand it, and take responsibility for helping the child to manage it well.

Secondly, know that most children with ADHD eventually grow up into reasonably productive and reasonably happy adults. Just like everyone else. Do not allow the disorder-mongers and mental illness purveyors to convince you that your child is somehow a different species of child, doomed to failure and unhappiness. That is also pure unadulterated nonsense.

Each child with ADHD is a unique individual, with unique strengths and weaknesses, and a unique personality. Each will make his or her own way in life, to different levels of success and happiness.

Thegoalforparentsandeducatorsistohelpthose children with ADHD manage age-appropriate responsibilities, learn in school, get along with and make friends with their peers, and mature along with their peers as they get older. Just like all children.

Children with ADHD need the same basic things that all children need–and sometimes they need a little more. All children need structure and routines, but children with ADHD may need it more. All children need to be taught organization skills, but kids with ADHD may need to work harder and longer at developing them. All children need consistency concerning study schedules, morning routines, and bedtime routines, but many children with ADHD need it more.

Developing efficient systems of organization and other productivity skills does not end when childhood ends. That is an ongoing process

that lasts into adulthood for all people who care about being productive. The goal with all children, whether or not they have ADHD, is to help them build a solid foundation before they reach adulthood. Below are some strategies that could be helpful.

Maintain Realistic Expectations and Provide Appropriate Assistance

One of the leading gurus of the disorder model of ADHD decided a long time ago that children with ADHD are developmentally and emotionally delayed by an average of three years compared to their peers. This now appears to be accepted as gospel truth by many professionals working in the ADHD field.

In my experience, this is painting with a brush that is much too broad. Some children are slower to mature, many are not, and some are precocious and more mature than their age peers.

Some (not all) children with ADHD are indeed slower to develop emotional self-control, but that comes with the territory of having a high level of emotionality as part of one's basic

biology. Some children take longer to develop organization and time management skills, which comes with the biological territory of having a poor sense of time and poor sense of the passage of time.

These are common features of ADHD biology, and not necessarily "developmental delays" that cause any significant problems. As every parent knows, different children develop at their own pace in different areas of growth and development. It is not a race. Stereotyping children with ADHD as being three years behind their peers in emotional and cognitive development is inaccurate and terribly unhelpful.

What is important in parenting or educating any child is to take the maturity level and the skills level of that particular child into consideration. It is frustrating for all involved to expect a child to do what that child is not yet capable of doing. For example, one of the most unhelpful messages to parents from educators is that "he (or she) is old enough to do that by himself (or herself) by now."

No, it is not a matter of age or maturity level. If a particular child needs more help to get more consistent with routines and other organization skills, for example, then provide what that child needs for as long as necessary to develop and maintain those behavioral skills.

Co-ordinate Strategies and Services with Teachers, Principals, and School Counselors

The large majority of children with ADHD do not need special education services. As mentioned above, some will benefit from more individualized attention and behavior skills training. Often this can be done on an informal basis, particularly with children in the early grades, based on discussions between parents and teachers.

If a broader range of services or more structured plans might be needed, request to have the school conduct a formal 504 evaluation. This involves an assessment to determine the child's educational needs with input from a team of the school staff. Parents contribute to this process along with teachers, school counselors, the principal or other administrators, and possibly the school psychologist if psychological or

psychoeducational testing is called for.

Helping a Child Manage Clutter

Assign every object in a child's room a designated "home" location. This is where things are put when they are not being used.

The Magic of Routines

All children benefit from routines to promote consistent behavior. Not every activity needs to be (or should be) turned into a routine. They are most helpful for accomplishing common tasks (e.g., brush your teeth before going to bed) and keeping daily life manageable. Below are some of the most basic and helpful routines.

MOST PEOPLE WITH ADHD have a binary sense of time. The most urgent sense of time, and honestly, the only one that feels relevant, is best described as "now." Anything that does not fall under the current experience of "now" falls into a distant and vague notion of "later." This goes a long way towards explaining why people live in the moment and react to the immediate. Time does not have much "depth" to it. "Now" is the only priority, the rest is a foggy unknown that doesn't get much if any attention.

This biological explanation does not mean that people with ADHD cannot manage time well. ADHD should never be used as an excuse for failing to look ahead and plan well, or for habitually running late because of underestimating how long it takes to get somewhere. Individuals with ADHD can do well with managing time—it just takes a little extra work.

Improving one's sense of time and managing time well can be done with the help of a variety of systems and routines. The following are some examples.

Make Time Visual

Many people with ADHD report that their sense of time improves when they can "see" time. Actually, this phenomenon helps everyone, but individuals with ADHD get an even greater benefit from it.

Using some kind of planner, hard copy or digital is essential to making time visual. You want to be able to see your day, with all the hourly time blocks and all the items on your schedule. See your week. See your month. Making time visual

simply provides more perspective and makes time feel more "real." It makes planning easier, including estimating and allocating time for tasks and projects.

Learn to Estimate Time Better (The 1.5 Rule)

Two factors work against people with ADHD when it comes to estimating time accurately. Luckily, both factors can be overcome with an awareness and some coping skills. First, as mentioned above, time awareness does not come naturally. This is pure biology. Second, in my experience, many people with ADHD are eternal optimists. This is part of their emotionality.

The result is chronic underestimating how long things take due to over-optimistic expectations. Sure, Merle says to herself, I can finish that paper in three hours–although realistically, it will take six or more. Sure, Randall says to himself, I can get to my dentist appointment in 15 minutes–although realistically, it will take 30 minutes. This explains why Merle turns in papers late, and why Randall is habitually 10 or 15 minutes late. Even though it frustrates them, it keeps happening.

The solution to solving the problem of underestimating time is to not trust your sense of time. It does not matter how smart or responsible you are. If you have ADHD, chances are that your brain will fool you and you will underestimate how much time you need to (fill in the blank). And the next thing you know, you are late for your dentist's appointment—again!

An elegantly simple strategy for estimating time more accurately is to use the 1.5 rule. However, much time you think you need to get something done or to get somewhere, multiply that time by 1.5. If you think you need two hours to write that report, schedule three hours. If you think you need 30 minutes to get somewhere, give yourself 45 minutes.

The 1.5 rule works so well for people who use it and stick with it, it's almost spooky. The only way it doesn't work is if people stop using it. In order to work consistently, it must become a routine and be used consistently.

Experience being the best teacher, some people find that 1.5 times still leaves them a bit short. In that situation, it is perfectly fine to convert it to a 2.0 rule. What works for you is

what works for you. This principle also applies to academic accommodations, for example, when requesting extended time testing. Most people do fine with 1.5 times, but some need 2.0 times.

Use Planners and Calendars like A General

Time management cannot be done efficiently without using a planner. This applies to all people with a busy lifestyle, and it is critical for most people with ADHD. Without a planner, a realistic schedule, and some consistent routines, people tend to be scattered and jump from one thing to another. That is the recipe for being unproductive. That old saying about inefficiency–"The best way to get nothing done is to try to do everything at once"—becomes a way of life.

CHAPTER - 6

THE ADHD ADVANTAGE

Parenting a child with ADHD requires flexibility, invention, and a great deal of patience, not only with your child but also with yourself. While you will be going on to help your child using the strategies this book discusses, it is important to realize that ADHD requires long-term management. Yes, the symptoms will improve, but the disorder will not just go away overnight. In some cases, it can be a lifelong condition. So, think of being the parent of a child with ADHD as an exciting adventure with myriad challenges, opportunities...and happy surprises!

Take Mariah, a doctor. Her child, Jackson, was diagnosed with ADHD, and Mariah found it difficult to understand and empathize with his behaviors. He was clearly very bright, but he did not do the work expected of him and

performed poorly in middle school. In high school, he discovered the magic of physics and understood the subject so well that he excelled in it. But even though Mariah did not always relate to what Jackson was interested in, she acknowledged and accepted that he was going to do things in a very different way than she had. While Mariah went directly to medical school after college, Jackson decided to move to rural Maine for several years to work as an organic farmer. At the same time, he took pre-med courses and eventually enrolled in a scientific research, graduate program several years after graduating from college. Along the way, he made friends with a disparate group of people, learned how to farm, and brought real-life knowledge to his study of science.

Like Jackson, many children with ADHD make surprising choices. If parents stay flexible and open-minded, however, they can support and guide their children as they make exciting discoveries about their own talents and interests.

When Parents Also Have ADHD

If you also have ADHD, it may make parenting your child with ADHD feel doubly hard, but your experiences may also make you more understanding and receptive to what your child is going through. In the last several years, the world of ADHD has changed a lot. There is a much greater understanding of the condition and strategies, medications, and other interventions that help children with ADHD perform better at school and at home. And for many more children are properly diagnosed now than in years past, they can receive the help they need.

Some adults with ADHD may not have been diagnosed when they were younger, and they may have grown up without understanding ADHD or having others around them understand what they were going through. If you can relate to this, be aware that your child's experiences will most likely be different from yours; there is a greater appreciation and understanding of ADHD today. You don't need to worry that your child's experiences will replicate your own. It is certainly helpful to self-reflect, but you'll want

to avoid projecting any negativity from your past onto your child. The condition may be the same, but each individual is different.

If you grew up with ADHD, you likely have a greater sensitivity to your child's challenges and experiences. You may also be aware that there are benefits to having the condition. In fact, you can use your own sense of experimentation and flexibility to try out and adapt strategies to help your child.

David Neeleman, an entrepreneur who started three commercial airlines, including JetBlue, has spoken publicly about growing up with ADHD. He dropped out of college and went on to found Morris Air, which was later sold to Southwest Airlines. Neeleman used his restlessness and sense of adventure to his advantage. He constantly rode on his own airplanes, making sure they were comfortable and engaging to his customers. He's the smart guy who decided to install TV screens in the back of each seat because he understood that people needed to be entertained as they flew. Having ADHD made him more inventive and, in part, helped him rethink the way a commercial

airline treats its customers.

Parenting Principles

As you help your child develop strategies to work with ADHD, there are several principles to keep in mind. These principles will help you guide your child in a realistic and caring way, with an understanding that there is no cure-all for ADHD. The guidance you provide can help your child work at their own pace toward understanding the condition and working with it.

Practice Patience

All parents need patience, and this quality is particularly important for parents of children with ADHD. While it is natural for parents to want to "solve" their children's problems and "cure" their ADHD, the reality for most children is that they need time to develop. Studies conducted by the NIMH and others have shown that children with ADHD will develop in similar ways as that of their peers, except in brain development, where they lag behind about three years. These studies suggest that parents can be assured that their children will eventually

develop the necessary organizational, planning, and judgment skills exercised by children without ADHD. But, the slower trajectory toward maturation means extra patience and an eye on long-term development, rather than quick fixes, may be necessary.

Keep an Eye on The Long Term

This is related to patience. Parents should understand that even though they are taking steps to help their child, they might not see immediate results. Change and maturation require time, and children may develop more slowly in some areas than in others. They may experience occasional setbacks, but these bumps in their development do not mean that they won't eventually have all of the tools they require for a rich and productive life.

Ask Others for Help

While it is natural for parents to want to help their children on their own, it really does "take a village" to raise all kids, particularly those with learning differences. In other words, reach out to a community of people who have children with ADHD, whether online or in your area, for

advice and support. It is a positive reflection of your parenting style to enlist the help of adults your child interacts with, including not only teachers, but also perhaps coaches, tutors, doctors, therapists, and religious leaders. Enlisting the help of others may be particularly important as your child enters adolescence, a period when children are often less receptive to what their parents have to say.

Externalize Rewards

As ADHD expert Russell Barkley, PhD, noted in Taking Charge of ADHD, children with ADHD may not internalize motivation as other children do over time, and they may need external motivations and supports to change their behavior. This does not mean that parents need to bribe children, but it does mean that parents need to consider what children with ADHD value, such as playing video games or sports, and use these interests as rewards for children's completion of more mundane activities. While many parents want children to carry out tasks just because it is the right thing to do, children with ADHD may need to be externally motivated until they can develop

a more intrinsic sense of what they need to do overtime. Several strategies in this book suggest external rewards to keep your child motivated.

Recognize Positive Behaviors

Children with ADHD often require constant feedback. Be sure to recognize what your child is doing well, even if it's just part of a larger task or something trivial. For example, while most school-age children can get dressed and eat breakfast independently, many children with ADHD need to be praised for each step of the process, so they complete on their own— for instance, putting on their socks or tying their shoes without help, or sitting at the table for ten minutes without fidgeting. Though many parents may feel that children should not be praised for tasks that are expected of them at a certain age, children with ADHD need this praise to motivate them to keep completing these tasks on their own. It may feel strange to praise children who are still developing skill sets that their peers have already incorporated—or which parents think are easy—but it is necessary to keep children with ADHD moving toward independence. Big

leaps can happen in very unexpected time frames, and little changes happen all the time; be unconditionally supportive of your child, and notice when they succeed regardless of how trivial the accomplishment may seem to you.

Break Down Tasks and Directions into Smaller Parts

Children with ADHD often need longer tasks and directions broken down into smaller, easier to manage pieces. Parents, teachers, and other caregivers should avoid assuming that a child with ADHD will understand how to break down longer tasks on their own. For example, in the morning, your child may need a list of each task they need to complete. An example might look like this: (1.) Take your clothes out of your drawer. (2.) Put on your clothes, starting with your socks, etc. School assignments need to be broken down similarly. Also, specific times for completion need to be assigned, as many children with ADHD do not have an intrinsic sense of how to plan or complete tasks within a certain time frame.

Communicate with Teachers and Other Professionals

Be open and honest with your child's teachers and other adults who work with your child, such as camp counselors. Children with ADHD have a legal right to special accommodations at school, including an Individualized Education Program (IEP), to help them succeed. However, many parents attempt to conceal an ADHD diagnosis, fearing that their child will be stigmatized. If they are not aware of the diagnosis, teachers and others in teaching and caregiving roles may assume a child is being willfully defiant or disruptive. If you communicate honestly about what your child is facing, this information will help teachers work with your child. Parents should not ask teachers to excuse their children from assignments. Instead, they should strategize with teachers about how to help their child complete the schoolwork.

Avoid Comparing Children to Others, Including Siblings

It can sometimes be difficult for parents who have children with different needs and developmental trajectories not to compare

their children to their siblings or peers. Children with ADHD already have an acute sense of not measuring up, and these types of comparisons, when shared with children, do not tend to motivate them. Comparisons to try to show your child with ADHD how they should behave can frustrate them further and lead to less self-confidence in working toward developing the skills they need.

Keep in Mind the Particular Challenges of Girls With ADHD

While all children with ADHD may find that their symptoms interfere with positive social interactions, girls with ADHD may run afoul of cultural stereotypes about the ways they should behave. For example, they may be considered odd, socially distractible, too brusque, bossy, or other qualities that society—including many children, parents, and teachers—are not taught to celebrate in girls. If you have a daughter with ADHD

Take Advantage of ADHD's Benefits and Energy

While there is no doubt that ADHD presents challenges, it also can confer a great sense of creativity, high energy, and often the considerable charm. The old adage, "feed the hungry bee," is a good mantra for parents. Find what your child likes to do, and encourage them to do it. For example, let's say your child loves working with tools or taking things apart

CHAPTER - 7

MANAGING ADHD BEHAVIOR
AWAY FROM HOME

ADHD behavior in the outside world is crucial. It can be dangerous to travel. For a fact, if your child goes outside limits and does damage to the property of others, the result may be costly. Even if you do not curtail the ADHD actions of your child, you risk not fulfilling your errands and upsetting strangers. When she handled herself, it would be fine, so how can you get that to happen?

Problems in The Car

The new relationship you build with your child will help immensely wherever you go, but during car rides, certain unusual issues that arise. It is both aggravating and risky to drive if your kid is misbehaving. You may be in a rush sometimes, and if your daughter doesn't want to help, she will ruin anything.

Solutions

You want your daughter to put on her seat belt without being told to do so, but if she's upset with something else, she may refuse. It makes better sense to look into the source of her annoyance than to focus only on her lack of compliance. Because the back seat can be lonely, by being proactive, you can also avoid negative attention. In a conversation, you can include your daughter, pack items of interest to her, or play a game with her to make the trip less lonely and boring.

When, when driving, your child starts a commotion, you may be worried about health. You may need to find a place for the car to rest and wait for it to settle down. Yeah, maybe you're late, but it's your best option. Let your child know, "Seeing more than one child ride with you is safe to drive only if we sit in our seats and get along." When you return to the lane, though, make sure the kids stop fighting and do something else, even if it just looks out the window. If they are not distracted from the conflict, the fighting can resume quickly.

Who Sits Where?

When there is constant disagreement over the seating arrangement in the car, apply the same techniques that you would use to minimize conflict within the household; help the kids figure out the sharing system they want to use. Do this before your next trip: ask the kids if they have any suggestions to fix the problem at a time when everyone is calm. Every child may have a special seating choice, but as long as the kids find out what works for them, everything is going to be fine. Make sure that their program correctly informs them, or it is unlikely to be effective, who has first preference at specific times. You don't want to keep track of whose turn it's for the seat you want.

Using the Bathroom

Trips are often long, and access to a toilet is not always easy. Your daughter may insist that she doesn't have to go to the bathroom until you go, but she may start complaining that she has to use the toilet shortly after she leaves. You should pause to comply easily, but try to find a solution that reduces the discomfort if the situation is routine. Let her know: "It's a long

trip, and finding a bathroom will be hard. Want to use the bathroom now to make you more relaxed while we're driving?" If she says no, you might add,' We'd be happy to wait for you,' as a way to make her rethink.

Help your child get into the bathroom routine before leaving. Model what you'd like her to do and ask if she'd like to take a turn. Start the journey, whether or not she is going. There may be a considerable difficulty if events play poorly, but try to stay relaxed as she pays attention to her own pain. She will eventually learn that she's better off modeling your actions, and you're not going to have to say a thing about it.

Problems in The Store

If you're looking for something she likes, your daughter may be very cooperative. But when she feels compelled to buy for others, her actions may be dramatically different. As is often the case, once she lacks the authority to determine what happens, the ADHD conduct of your daughter is sparked and intensified.

Solutions

If you're in a good mood, your child will behave more, so you have a significant influence. Talking about the favorite topics of discussion for your child can also help make unnecessary shopping less annoying. But most notably, if your child has more insight into what is going on, your child will probably comply more. If you're shopping for food, for example, you might ask her when she wants to help you decide what to get. Older kids might be happy to help you find bargains. Others may want to read the list of groceries or push the cart.

The bottom line is that when you and your child get along positively and share authority, ADHD behavior will be less frequent. Try to find the "sweet spot" where you get enough space for her to fit you easily so that you can complete the order. This is hard to achieve, but it can be achieved, and during shopping excursions, this has the biggest long-term effect on the rate of ADHD behavior.

Resolving Public Misbehavior

When you're out and about, things may not always go smoothly, so what do you do if your child acts up? If necessary, you should disregard or avoid the actions, but encouraging it to be loud and disruptive is not always acceptable to others. There may also be dangers when she's exuberant in public places that you don't want to play out.

Sadly, once your conduct is disrespectful or dangerous, you may have to physically stop your child or leave the store. In some situations, after a short time, it may be possible to re-enter the shop if your child settles down and you feel assured that when you return to the store, all will be optimistic.

Still, however, you might have to go back. It is crucial for your child to understand that her behaviors have a ripple effect in these circumstances. Such negative side effects can be illustrated. For starters, "Because we haven't done our shopping, we're going to have to go back later, and I'm not going to be able to make the dessert I was preparing of tonight." If the problem goes on, you might want to go one step

farther. You might suggest that your daughter spend some of her own money to pay for the return trip, pointing out the positives of this option (e.g., this compensates others for having inconvenienced them, and it might mitigate their difficult feelings against her). When she offers reimbursement, everyone benefits.

Like when dealing with hygiene issues, you might also ask your child if she'd like to stay home next time and use some of her own money to pay someone to keep her company. She thus carries some of the burden of refusing to satisfy the family agenda. Offer her choices, but also let her know that it may cost her some decisions.

Peer Relationships

Is your child accusing other kids of achieving a sense of superiority? Trying to "buy" friends by giving away personal items, displaying low self-esteem? Should she whine of mistreatment in order to get you to run her defense? Will she always sit on the playground by herself or just play with kids out of the common circle? If so, you might want to change it. You want a fun social life for your child and feel comfortable

interacting with a variety of people.

Misbehaving with Peers

Quite often, her conduct becomes excessive when a child with ADHD meets another rambunctious child. If she behaves stupidly and doesn't try to meet standards, she stops feeling inferior, and when she plays with another cap tester, there is no loss. There is power in numbers, and when she teams up with a "bad friend," your daughter gathers influence and leverage.

Solutions

You can try to keep your child away from other kids who act out. This can, however, give your child the impression of being weak and easily manipulated. Another approach is to make her realize why she is mistaken and help her handle what happens when she faces negative influences successfully. This approach sends her the impression that in her setting, she will show herself and bring about change. She will see herself as a leader with good sense. You might say, "Your friend might be clever enough to imitate you when you're playing together."

You might also ask your daughter how she feels about getting in trouble and raise the question, "How do you want others to see you?" You can help her work out what to do when others push the envelope to find out if she's scared that if she doesn't join, others will make fun of her.

They may also question whether the cap checking is acceptable because the tricks may be misplaced ways of gaining attention or forms of weakening authority. Let your child know that addressing her problem behavior with her peers has a key advantage: taking them on family excursions makes it fun.

Doubting Acceptability

If your daughter doubts, she's reasonable to others, she will find it harder to act fairly. Perhaps when she clowns around, she encourages others to grin, but the unfortunate side effect is that she gets attention for immature behavior. She briefly takes advantage of habits that will inevitably not serve her well. If that's the case, you might say, "Do you believe you're going to have to show off or do something dumb to make people like you?" Then ask, "How is this going to work for you?" When she thinks it goes

poorly, inquires, "I wonder if there are other ways to attract them?" You want to maintain your child's great sense of humor, but you don't want her to be crazy or dumb. She has many qualities that other people will admire, and you want her to bring out her best foot. Her actions with ADHD that diminish significantly when she is socially comfortable and confident that she is a friendly person. Additionally, her choice of friends will probably change if she feels good about herself.

Supporting Social Development

If your child is on the younger side, she'll probably repeat a lot of habits she experiences with other adults within the family. If she is demanding and possessive with you, with her playmates, she may also be demanding and possessive. When family members manipulate or disrespect her, or others give her a hard time, she can overreact or display fear. It is important to nurture habits that fit well with non-family members for these reasons. If you want her to communicate, accept social boundaries, and conduct with her peers assertively, improve her ability to connect within the group.

It is also helpful to give your child an opportunity to interact with other kids while encouraging their social development. So, she's going to increase her social skills. Encourage her effort and scheduling by saying "Let me know when you want to bring someone over so that we can make arrangements for a play date."

CHAPTER - 8

IMPROVING THE SOCIAL SKILLS OF CHILDREN WITH ADHD

During a child's development phase, some skills are quantifiable—language skills, math skills, etc. But what about the softer skills which, like social skills, do not come as naturally? ADHD kids also find it difficult to make friends and establish relationships. Some parents wonder how social skills can be developed, but often don't know where to start.

Children with ADHD are no different than children without—all of them want to be liked, want to be part of a group, and want to make friends—they just do not know-how. But all is not lost—there are strategies that you can do to help your child develop these social skills and competencies, as we will explore.

Increasing a Child's Social Awareness

According to the various research on ADHD, children with this disorder can be poor monitors of their own social behavior. They often do not have clarity on the awareness or understanding of social situations and the reactions they provoke from people around them. To them, a peer interaction went well, but, or to the other person, it did not.

To an ADHD child, an interaction with a peer may have gone well, but it did not. This is another example of an ADHD-related issue, where the ADHD child cannot accurately 'read' social situations, self-monitor themselves, and adjust their actions and behaviors according to the social setting. These skills would need to be taught directly to them.

Teach Skills Directly and Practice, Practice, Practice

Learning from past experiences also makes it a little harder when it comes to children with ADHD. Often, they react without thinking, but one of the ways to remedy this would be to constantly provide feedback immediately

whenever a child's behavior is inappropriate, or they have had social miscues. Roleplay is an extremely effective and helpful way of shaping, teaching, and practicing positive social skills and providing the child with ways to deal with difficult situations, such as bullying and teasing.

As a parent, you can start by focusing on one or two main areas that your child struggles with the most when it comes to social interactions. This creates a learning process that is not too overwhelming both for the child learning and parent teaching.

Often, children with ADHD have problems with the fundamentals of social exchanges such as:

- Starting and maintaining a conversation

- Interacting with people in a proper way

- Personal distance when talking

- Giving and receiving input

- Listening and asking for ideas

- Taking turns talking in a conversation

- Showing interest

- Negotiating and resolving a conflict

Speaking using a normal tone

Identify your child's social rules and behaviors clearly and give them information. Practice these prosocial abilities repeatedly. With immediate rewards, this will form positive behaviors.

Building Friendship Growth Opportunities

For elementary and preschool children, playdates offer a great opportunity for parents to model and coach positive peer interactions for them. For the child, they would be able to practice these new skills. You can set up these playtimes with one or two friends at a time—keep it minimal rather than having a large group of friends as this may be overwhelming for the child and for you. Plan playtime to be the most effective for your child.

Consider yourself as your child's "friendship mentor." Consider carefully how long a playdate takes and select activities that are most interesting for your child.

The older the child gets, friendships and peer relationships become more complicated but continue to remain involved in your child's life and help them facilitate interactions that are positive for themselves. For a kid who struggles socially, middle and high school years can be harsh. It would be good if the child can have a least one or two good friends throughout the years of school that can often be the child's support system rather than having a large group of friends.

Socially alienated middle-or secondary school students who face constant rejection may feel desperate to become members of any peer group—including those with adverse impact.

Another way to foster positive peer relationships outside of school is to get involved in groups within the community, such as Indian Guides, Boy Scouts, Girl Scouts, Girls Who Code, Rotary Club for kids, sports teams, and art groups, for example. When getting your children do join these clubs and teams, ensure that group leaders or mentors know about ADHD and create an environment that is both encouraging and constructive for your child. This is extremely

helpful in the long run.

Don't be worried or afraid to share information about your child's condition with kindergarten, coaches, and parents in the community, so you know what's going on with your child and who's spending time with your child. Withholding information will only make things worse. The peer group of a child and the features of the group affect the individuals in the group strongly.

Empowering the Peer Status of your Child through School

Peer groups are important for children, but the downside is that once they put a label on your child because of their lack of social skills, it can be hard to break away from this reputation. Having a reputation, especially one that isn't 'cool,' can become obstacles to your child. Negative peer labels are commonly established when the child is in early to middle school and this reputation does not fade away easily, even though the child develops positive social skills. This is one of the main reasons why it is extremely crucial for parents to collaborate with the school and their child's teachers, mentors,

and coaches to address any effects.

Lessening or stopping these negatives impacts can be done through establishing a positive working relationship with your child's —this is just one such example. Inform them about the strengths and desires of your child as well as what they struggle with. You can also share any approaches that you find helpful in focusing on the areas of weakness of your child.

When forming social preferences about their peers, young children often look to their teacher. A teacher's presence, warmth, acceptance, patience, and gentle direction can be an excellent model for the peer group and it also influences the child's social status. The teacher plays an important role in finding other ways to draw positivity and positive attention to the ADHD child.

In the presence of the other children in the school, one way to do this is to give the child special roles and obligations. As a teacher, you can make sure that these responsibilities can result in the child feeling success, and this can, in turn, develop feelings of acceptance within the classroom as well as feelings of confidence,

self-esteem, and self-worth in the self-conscious child.

This also gives opportunities for the peer group to view the child in a positive and encouraging light, which also helps to stop the group process of peer rejection. It can also help to promote social acceptance by pairing the child with a caring "buddy" in the classroom.

Setting Up Accommodations in School and at Home

The benefits of having a good, working relationship with your child's teacher is enabling them or helping the teacher outfit ADHD techniques and methods in the classroom. This helps the child to better manage their symptoms. Working together with a teacher or an adult caregiver, therapist, or coach on effective approaches towards behavior management and social skills is the best and most practical solution.

Inform your child's teacher about the medication taken by your child and if they need to take it during school hours. Be sure to work closely with the child's doctor as well because you may

need to give feedback on your child's responses, symptoms and so on both at home and school, so the doctor would be able to fine-tune and make adjustments to the child's medication along the way.

Friendship Development for the ADHD Child

It hurts the heart of a parent as they see their child struggling to make friends. Everything our kids need sometimes is a little encouragement to build relationships and avoid social slip-ups linked to ADHD. Here are some methods that will help:

How to Make Friends

- Getting to the cause of the problem—when it comes to ADHD children, they have very little idea on the perceptions their friends have on them, resulting in them making blunders without even knowing. You can help your child by helping them make sense of what happened. You could discuss the scenario, point out to them what went wrong, talk to them about what they can do the next time this happens again. Practice sensitivity and reduce any negative feedback.

- Congratulate them—when they do have successful interactions, congratulate your child. Watch them closely when they play with other kids so you can always keep a watchful eye and monitor the situation; they are in. You can intervene if there is a fight if your child starts telling fibs or if they are trying to attempt something dangerous to impress their friends.

- Team sports—Joining ADHD, friendly sports, or organized activities can open your children to possibilities that they never knew they had. Sports are also a good way to develop social skills, playing together, and positive attitudes.

- Try not to dive in-—when introducing a new sport to your ADHD child, speak with the coach first before going in for the first practice. Ask questions about whether your child who has ADHD is welcomed in the team. You can follow your child to meet the instructor, who may introduce your child to the game a little bit before the first practice.

- Take note of their competitive attitude— ADHD children can also have difficulty in

competitive play—Gloating on winning and crying on losing. If your child experiences these circumstances with difficulty, get them to learn other kinds of athletic ability that does not require doing it as a team, such as martial arts, running, gymnastics, golfing, and cycling.

- Trust that they will find their way—Children will eventually learn to cope and handle their situations and behaviors better, even when they have experienced social isolation. They will also learn how friendships work. When a child hits adolescence, they will act on the urge to fit in.

- Having just a few friends—this is something that needs to be drilled into the child. They do not need to be part of a huge group of friends or be invited into plenty of parties to be happy. Studies show that having close friends is what is needed for a child to be happy and to be socially developed and have self-confidence.

CHAPTER - 9

ADHD AT SCHOOL

Insisting on the structure in the child's day and having a routine is particularly helpful when your child starts school. Although it has nothing to do with his level of intelligence, your child who has ADHD is most likely to have a problem at school. Although ADHD is not technically a learning disability because of their behavioral problem, these children do struggle in the school system. When your child reaches the age of six and starts school, his symptoms become more apparent and they can also begin to have more of a negative effect on his life. He will have to worry about sitting still and paying attention in a classroom setting as well as remembering and sometimes following complex instructions. He will also have to deal with what is for some children the most difficult of all activities, which is interaction with other

children in social situations. It also forces the child to wake up early and to learn a whole new morning routine when he probably only just began to master the old one.

Work with the child's teachers and others at the school to help your child in controlling the disorder and getting as much from the school experience as possible. Helping your child to perform well at school is a big part of coping with ADHD in children. In order for your child to flourish at school, there must be a collaboration between the teachers, school administrators, and the parents of the child. Teachers should be well-informed about the child's condition so everyone can be on the same page regarding his needs. Your child will most likely need a great deal of help coping with life at school because he will find it difficult to sit still for long periods of time as school often requires. He may get up and walk around at inappropriate times and says inappropriate things. He may also have difficulty following complex directions needing everything to be explained most simply and clearly. Parents and teachers should work together to ensure that notes are taken and homework assignments are completed.

He will also forget to record the homework assignment and to prepare for the test. Because they aren't always paying attention, they may not know about upcoming activities unless they are written down in his notebook by the teacher. They will be distracted by things which other students in the class are doing or even thing that are going on outside.

Play an active role in your child's education. Request and attend meetings at his school with his teachers and school psychologists. Make sure that you are allowed to have input and to ask questions in the meeting. Find out if everyone is moving in the same direction regarding your child's education and if they are not, see what you can do to address the situation. You can also ask for the child's therapist to be present at meetings so that he or she can advise the teachers on the best way to get the most out of their time with the child.

Be prepared to spend many an evening doing homework with your child, who will most likely take a lot longer to complete his homework than the other children in his class and who will need you to help him stay focused and to get rid of distraction.

You should also learn as much as you can about your child's legal rights regarding his education. There are laws in some countries which state that your child cannot be discriminated against for an education because he has a disorder. They also state that provisions should be made for that disorder in the delivery of education, in that if a special education teacher is needed, then one should be provided. The child will qualify for these special considerations once it is proved that his disorder limits his ability to function at school. In short, do as much as you can ensure that your child receives the best education possible so that he can reach his full potential.

Ask the teacher to keep you informed about what takes place in the classroom, whether your child is being disruptive or not. Getting regular updates keeps you, the parent informed, and able to tell if your child needs further therapy or other types of exercise.

If he isn't already sitting up front, ask the teacher to put him up front where she can tell if he is paying attention and pull him back when he stops and starts daydreaming or gets

distracted by something else.

It is also important to let the teachers and school officials know that you have expectations for your child as far as his education is concerned. Make it clear what your goals and objectives are and work with them to achieve them. Get input from the teachers regarding how reasonable those expectations are and welcome their advice and recommendations, but be alert for signs that the school has given up on your child and speak to the teachers about it right away. If both teams are not working in tandem, the child will not flourish in that atmosphere. Be careful not to compare your child to others. His life is not a competition. Just ensure that he lives up to his full potential.

There should be a special place established where homework is done. Make it a quiet area with no distractions, as children with ADHD are very easily distracted. The television should be off or out of hearing and if there are other children, they should be in another room if possible. If there are small children in the home, have the other parent or other family members keep them organized until homework time is

over. Make it clear to the child that he must record his homework assignments, as they are likely to forget to do this.

While you will need to help with homework, resist the urge to do it for him, although you might assist by making the instructions simpler so that he can follow them. It might help to divide the assignments into more manageable portions, so your child does not feel overwhelmed. Take breaks if you need to so that he has an opportunity to refocus.

As a parent of a child with ADHD, you would probably have to buy extra school supplies such as pens, pencils and erasers, because Kids with ADHD tend to forget things and are usually not very organized.

Bullying

While many parents of children with ADHD are teased about their condition at school, research appears to show that children with ADHD are quite likely to become bullies at school. There can be various reasons for this. Children with ADHD often have a lot of aggression and they also often suffer from poor social skills.

Because of their inability to fully pay attention and focus on what's going on, the child with ADHD also struggle academically, when you combine all these things the child must feel a lot of frustration and may choose to show it by bullying other children. Because they do not feel much empathy, they would feel no guilt over taking advantage of another child in an effort to stop feeling bad about themselves and their inability to fit in. The medication would not make a difference in this scenario, as the stimulants usually given to children with ADHD do not weaken the aggression they feel.

Parents can help to decrease or stop the bullying habits of their children by first letting them know in a calm and unemotional tone as possible that they have been informed about the behavior. Then they have to impress upon their child, who most likely feels no remorse, that while they continue to love him unconditionally, his behavior is unacceptable. Let him know that if the behavior continues, there will be consequences just as there have always been for breaches of good behavior. The parent should also work with the child's teacher to try to find something for the child to do at

school to occupy his time and give him a sense of responsibility and purpose. He could have a role with one of the sporting teams, tidying up the locker room or do simple clerical tasks for one of the teachers or school administrators. He will feel less need to work off aggression if he is busy completing a task that he knows he has been entrusted to carry out.

Another proactive action would be to try and take him out of the situations where he is likely to bully other children, such as during the lunch break or after school. Teachers can ensure that the child spends this time in a location that is supervised. If you want to go closer to the source of the problem, you can sign your child up for counseling or anger management session to teach him to control his emotions before they get to the point of violence, or if you feel you can handle it yourself, you can engage him in role-playing sessions where you teach him to respond to situations without resorting to bullying. Encourage him to talk about how he is feeling instead of acting out.

What you don't want to do when you find out that your child may be bullying, is to lose your

temper and scream and shout at your child. Never resort to a violent means of punishment such as spanking because that would just confuse the child because how can you teach that violence is unacceptable by being violent yourself? You do not want to blame yourself either. Your child is not bullying other children because you failed as a parent. Don't react by making excuses for his behavior and finding fault with your own, that would be counterproductive as it would not do anything to alleviate the behavior and will probably make it worse.

It is interesting to note that although children with ADHD tend to become bullies with more frequency than other children, they are also children most likely to have been bullied at some point. When this happens, it usually leads to an increase in their symptoms, so talk to your child if you hear or believe he is being bullied before he gets to the point of frustration that causes him to be bullied himself. Talk to the teachers at his school about what is happening so they can take action, if needed, move him out of the situation. Be there for him, so he does not lose his self-esteem.

CHAPTER - 10

BEHAVIOR THERAPY

Behavior therapy, also called behavioral modification, is a common type of mental health counseling (psychotherapy) that replaces negative habits with positive ones. Its primary focus is the alteration of the external environment and the physiological function of the internal environment to cause behavior change. It addresses specific problem behaviors by increasing positive attention, establishing routines at home, and structuring time. Cognitive behavior therapy is a similar therapy and offshoot of behavior therapy. By contrast, cognitive therapy focuses on thinking as the factor that will create change. It helps children with ADHD recognize inaccurate thinking patterns so that they can more effectively assess challenging situations and respond to them in a more positive manner. It is particularly helpful

to improve social skills and for parent training. Because these two forms of psychological therapy are more similar than dissimilar, they will not be differentiated for the purpose of this text; rather, the term behavior therapy will be used.

Behavior therapy is based on the theories of classical and operant conditioning. Classical conditioning suggests that all behavior is learned, and faulty learning (conditioning) causes abnormal behavior. To correct the abnormal or negative behavior, an individual must be taught the correct or acceptable behavior. In other words, a response to a situation is learned and repeated through association, and behavior therapy aims to disconnect the situational association with the negative learned response. Operant conditioning utilizes reinforcement, punishment, shaping (the gradual training of a person to respond a specific way to situations by reinforcing the desired response), and modeling (learning by imitating what has been observed) techniques to alter behavior. In the end, the goal is to teach and reinforce positive behaviors and eliminate negative learned behaviors and responses.

Behavior Therapy Techniques

Positive Reinforcement

This technique works well for young children who require immediate gratification for positive behaviors. Small rewards—treats, stickers, TV time, etc.—are provided to the child in exchange for compliance with requests.

Reward System

This technique is more suited for older children who understand long-term goals and rewards. As part of this system, a chart with goals is placed in a visible location. When the child completes a goal, a mark is placed next to the goal, and when all goals are achieved, a bigger reward is offered.

Time-out

Time-outs are best reserved for a cooling-off period rather than a punishment. If the child is losing his or her temper or becoming frustrated, ask the child to sit in a quiet place for a few minutes without distractions.

Withholding Privileges

This technique involved removing a privilege when the child misbehaves and should be reserved for behaviors that are dangerous or very troublesome.

Token Economy

A token economy involves earning points for positive behavior and losing points for negative behavior. At the end of an agreed upon time, the child may receive a prize

Behavior therapy is a vital part of treatment for ADHD, but it is most effective when collaboration exists between the therapist and the prescriber. It is intended to teach children behavioral, social, and academic skills that are useful in managing ADHD symptoms throughout life. It can improve ADHD symptoms as well as the child's relationship with peers and family members. Medication addresses ADHD on the neurological level to regulate the brain and may be effective in reducing impulsivity and inattention, but it generally doesn't result in the child learning positive behaviors to substitute for the negative ones. For example,

the medication may effectively prevent the child from hitting his younger sibling, but it will not teach him what to do instead of hitting. Behavior therapy provides positive alternative behaviors to use.

Behavior therapy, or parent training, can also be beneficial for the parents of children with ADHD. During these sessions, parents learn techniques that can be used to motivate children to change negative behaviors. Parents are taught to set specific, simple, and clear goals for their children. Achievement of these goals is reinforced by a reward system, positive reinforcement, time-outs, withholding privileges, or a token economy. In addition, therapists help parents understand what influences their children's behavior and how to adjust their parenting accordingly to more effectively motivate and reinforce positive behaviors.

Sample Daily Routine—School-Age Children:

This sample daily routine is meant to be a guide to help you establish the structure and a predictable daily routine for your child with ADHD. It is best to put the routine in writing

(clear and brief wording) in a conspicuous place for your child to refer to and follow. Don't throw in the towel after a few days or even a few weeks just because the routine isn't "working." You need to help your child with ADHD understand that this is not a temporary adjustment, but a permanent way of life that will help him be more successful. Many children with ADHD need incremental time warnings, so you may want to use phrases like "you have five more minutes…" If you are committed, firm and patient (you may need to teach the routine over and over until they do it out of habit) establishing a routine can help improve efficiency, make daily activities more manageable, reduce overall family stress, and strengthen family relationships.

7:00 a.m. WAKE UP

Stick with the same wake-up time every day, even on weekends, to make mornings easier and encourage a natural circadian rhythm. Wake younger children with a gentle touch. Older children can use an alarm. If your child wakes up before the designated time, allow him to play in his room quietly without any screen time. As a visual reminder of when he is permitted to get

up, consider a dual-color nightlight (available online at places like Amazon.com) that turns green when it is okay to wake up the parents.

7:05 a.m. MORNING HYGIENE

Post a checklist that includes the steps to get ready for the day, such as "make your bed, put on clean clothes, wash face, and brush hair." It may be helpful to organize outfits (underwear, top, bottom, and socks) in a closet organizer identified by the days of the week (Sunday through Saturday). Allowing a child to help pick out his weekly outfits at the beginning of the week can help reduce the struggles of selecting an outfit in the morning or pulling out everything in the dresser to find his favorite Avengers t-shirt.

7:20 a.m. BREAKFAST

Offer two choices of healthy breakfast (with complex carbohydrates and high-quality protein). For, example "Choice number one for breakfast is; and choice number two for breakfast is." Avoid the "trigger" ingredients like refined sugar, food colorings, and additives. Don't forget any dietary supplements he takes

in the morning.

7:40 a.m. BRUSH TEETH

Consider brushing your teeth together, which can help keep him on task and ensure good hygiene.

7:45 a.m. EXIT—PUT ON SHOES

Keep backpack, shoes, and other outdoor gear by the door. Get shoes on (and a jacket and hat if necessary, for weather conditions).

7:50 a.m. TRAVEL TO SCHOOL

8:00 a.m. SCHOOL

2:50 p.m.

2:50 p.m. TRAVEL HOME/ENTRANCE

Ask about your child's day as you travel home. Hang up and put away all outside gear, shoes, and backpack by the door.

3:00 p.m. SNACK

Provide a healthy snack and let your child unwind after school. Children with ADHD often do well eat smaller, more frequent meals and snacks.

3:20 p.m. HOMEWORK OR CHORES

HOMEWORK: Establish a "homework area" where your child consistently sits (or stands) to do his homework. Have all the tools (pen or pencil, calculator, paper, etc.) ready and available in the homework area. Go through your child's backpack together and identify any homework, assignments, or notes that need to be taken care of. Reduce distractions in the homework area (TV, phone calls, activity, unnecessary noise). Play classical music for part of the homework time if desired. Be available to help your child with homework, answer questions, and supervise breaks (stretch, drink, jog in place, etc.). Some children may not be able to sustain their attention on homework for a continuous thirty minutes. Set a timer for 5, 10, or 15 minutes (age-appropriate) for 2-minute active breaks (dancing, jumping jacks, etc.). Praise your child when he puts forth his best effort and finishes required tasks. Waiting until the evening may create a battle, so after a snack is ideal. Set a specific amount of time to complete homework and then stop working on it.

CHORES: If your child has no homework or it is a day off from school, choose appropriate and specific tasks to complete as chores. Consider creating a weekly chore chart to establish consistency and a pattern of chores each day.

3:50 p.m. REVIEW HOMEWORK OR CHORES

Review your child's homework and calmly explain anything he needs to correct. Make sure to praise him for good work or efforts.

4:00 p.m. FREE TIME

Providing free play for activities such as outside play, sports, or other physical activity is as important as structured time. This could even include some limited screen time. However, the American Academy of Pediatrics urges parents to avoid TV viewing for children under age 2 and limit screen time to one or two hours daily for older children. Other experts suggest older children get no more than 1.5 hours of screen time daily—with a 1-hour limit even better. Perhaps a better option than screen time is to play with your child. Play-based interventions can improve ADHD symptoms and nurture a healthier parent-child relationship.

5:30 p.m. DINNER PREPARATION

Enlist the help of your child with age-appropriate dinner preparation steps (setting the table, making the salad, etc.). Giving them specific tasks to prepare for dinner helps establish a sense of responsibility.

6:00 p.m. DINNER

Serve a well-balanced meal. Engage your child and the rest of the family in conversation.

6:30 p.m. DINNER CLEAN UP

Involve your child in dinner age-appropriate dinner clean up (clear the table, put away leftovers, load the dishwasher, or dry dishes.

7:00 p.m. RELAXATION

After dinner should be a time for relaxing and winding down. This is a great time to read with your child or listen to calm music. If TV or a movie is watched, choose shows that are calm, not action thrillers or dramas. Avoid energizing activities like video games or active play. Play a board or card game, color together, draw pictures, or another activity that will promote a more relaxed state to get ready for bed. A

5-to 10-minute deep pressure (deeper or more pressure than a typical light massage) essential oil massage to the back and/or feet using essential oils.

8:00 p.m. EVENING SNACK

Allow your child to graze on healthy snacks when he may be hungriest (right before bed).

8:10 p.m. GET READY FOR BED

Create a detailed checklist of the activities your child should do to get ready for bed (shower or bathe, brush teeth, put on pajamas, put dirty clothes in the laundry hamper, and go to the bathroom).

8:30 p.m. BEDTIME

Maintain a regular sleep schedule and a consistent bedtime. Tuck your child in while singing a calming song, complimenting him on his successes that day, or whatever habitual bedtime routine you follow.

CHAPTER - 11

EFFECTIVE METHODS TO DEAL WITH ADHD

Grown-ups can oversee ADHD from numerous points of view. A portion of the couple is referenced underneath.

Through Coaching

Grown-up ADHD treatment includes something other than drugs. Drugs will assist patients with adapting, but they can't create abilities in individuals since they are not made to do as such. Medications may anyway make it simpler for ADHD sufferers to learn. At the point when individuals stop their medicine, the impacts may wear off; however, learned abilities don't dissipate inside meager air.

ADHD instructing assists patients with learning regular ideas. They figure out how to oversee themselves much more viably in their day by day lives. ADHD therapy depends on the past,

yet instructing depends on the present and future. Mentors for ADHD assist patients with building up their qualities instead of becoming frail. Mentors additionally assist patients with recognizing the issues that they experience the ill effects of.

Mentors likewise assist patients with creating certainty so they can fend off emerging clashes absent a lot of trouble. Patients more often than not have the hardest time adapting to their very own selves and this is the thing that mentors do. They assist them with growing increasingly confident.

Cognitive Behavioral Therapy (CBT)

Cognitive Based Therapy ought to be directed by either a specialist or a mentor who knows about grown-up ADHD treatment. This therapy is essential since it manages the past of a patient and causes him/her to reveal issues structure the past that blend with an individual's present working. It may turn into a troublesome issue if past issues are not managed.

Going to cognitive therapy ought not to be considered as an indication of shortcomings.

Rather, it is a positive sign that you are prepared to support yourself.

Adequate Diet

Medication, training, and therapy, but diet likewise impacts your condition on the off chance that you experience the ill effects of ADHD. Fundamentally, a grown-up experiencing ADHD incorporate protein in their eating routine that helps manufacture Dopamine. Your doctor may likewise assist you with arranging a solid eating routine on the off chance that you counsel them in regards to this issue. It is a great idea to incorporate natural products, vegetables, and nuts that help increment an individual's memory and these sorts of nourishment are not extremely overwhelming or swelling.

Exercise

Exercise doesn't mean one needs to exhaust themselves. It is only valuable to give three significant synapses a lift. Specialists have proposed that through exercise, grown-ups experiencing ADHD can successfully mitigate their pressure and wretchedness. It

has additionally been named as extraordinary compared to other non-medicinal approaches to treat the ADHD issue. Thousand years Medical Associates can assist you with managing ADHD when you request help.

Step by Step Instructions to Teach Kids With ADHD

The very idea of ADHD makes showing children with this issue amazingly troublesome. They have limited capacity to focus, an excess of vitality, and an inclination to carry on improperly without ever truly acknowledging they are doing it. Guardians and instructors have been approaching themselves for quite a long time how to teach kids with ADHD.

Since ADHD isn't a learning issue, there is nothing about the turmoil that makes it unnecessarily hard for children to learn. This is uplifting news! That implies that if you can persuade them to concentrate on an errand, they are completely equipped for holding what they have seen, heard, and done. The hardest piece of how to instruct kids with ADHD is getting them to concentrate on one undertaking long enough to realize what they have to realize.

Here are a few hints on the most proficient method to train kids with ADHD utilized by guardians, clinicians, doctors, and instructors everywhere throughout the world to assist us with teaching ADHD children.

Adjust your timetable to coordinate theirs as regularly as could be expected under the circumstances. After some time, you will start to see that children with ADHD will, in general, have a specific calendar to their states of mind unsurprising times of the day where they are particularly moldable versus times of the day where their vitality level is generally frenzied. Endeavoring to design exercises during their calm time and leisure time or physical action when their vitality is at its pinnacle will make the showing increasingly profitable for both of you.

A. Break up your educating plan. Some portion of figuring out how to instruct kids with ADHD is figuring out how to function with their issue, not show their issue to work with you. Since the greatest hindrance understudies experiencing ADHD face is their capacity to concentrate on an undertaking for any time span, separating these

errands into littler interims will make it simpler for them to succeed. These interims might be ten minutes, five minutes, or ten seconds, as long as they are inside the youngster's sensible abilities.

B. Transition gradually. Something therapists hear again and again with regards to children with ADHD is that they can't stay aware of the remainder of the family when it's an ideal opportunity to change exercises quit playing and come in to eat, for instance, or leave one store and travel to another. Getting things done can be a bad dream. If you can give your kid a lot of time to plan for the progress, be that as it may, telling them twenty minutes early and starting to make the essential changes five to ten minutes before you really need to, you'll see that you meet with less obstruction.

C. Keep learning dynamic and intuitive. One of the little-known mysteries in how to show kids with ADHD that is being utilized by guardians everywhere throughout the world (to the express objection to teachers) is the utilization of computer games. One multi-year old youngster with extreme ADHD had

the option to figure out how to peruse on a third-grade level since he consistently took an interest in web-based gaming encounters, where perusing was a need to stay aware of the gathering. Other children react well to instructive programming that still enables them to change landscape routinely, while still others do best have a grown-up working with them intelligently through hands-on rounds of catch, coordinating, or other expertise building practices that don't expect them to remain in their seats.

No, reassuring children to invest unnecessary measures of energy playing computer games or hopping around a room won't set them up forever spent secured away a work area, however, it very well may be an extraordinary method to show them the abilities they have to succeed and isn't that what makes a difference most?

Figuring out how to listen better with ADHD— An Act of Self-Love

One of my customers—I'll call him Jake—had a simple time making companions since he was active, clever, and well disposed of. He

experienced considerable difficulties keeping companions, however, due to his absence of listening abilities. He continually intruded. He would ask somebody an inquiry and, afterward, start searching for something additionally fascinating while the individual was replying. His concern wasn't with talking or being social; it was the listening that was so difficult. Jake wanted to have ADHD made it practically difficult to listen when somebody was looking at something that didn't generally intrigue him or influence him legitimately.

This may sound silly; however, building up our listening aptitudes is a demonstration of self-esteem. Why? Since we pass up so much when we can't tune in! If all we hear are our own considerations, we can't hear what our kid needs to explain to us or why our companion is feeling tragic or when a vocation or task needs to get wrapped up. We pass up cozy connections and different delights of life.

I realize that ADHD and consistent/quick-moving musings make it hard. A few people find that drug aides and others use different methodologies to remain centered. Here are

some fascinating activities to attempt. The practices beneath include mindfulness and tuning in to things we may not more often than not tune in to. They can be unwinding and charming if we approach them with interest and like a trial to attempt. The significant part isn't getting excessively disappointed if your contemplations interrupt. That is consummately typical and part of the procedure.

Practices to Improve Listening Skills

1. Begin to get mindful of what is happening within you when another person is talking. Is it true that you are eager, exhausted, or anxious? Perhaps you're not so much tuning in, however, simply sitting tight for an interruption so you can say something. Do you all of a sudden understand that you've been daydreaming and up to speed in your very own considerations or stresses? Do you interfere with on the grounds that you're apprehensive you'll overlook what you needed to state?

Check whether you can see when the demonstration of listening requires less exertion. Does it have to do with the individual who is talking? The clamor or articulation in

their voice? Improve when there is a passionate charge to the discussion or theme? Perhaps you listen well when there are hard outcomes on the off chance that you don't. How does nature influence your capacity?

At the point when you get an opportunity, record your revelations.

2. Develop your listening aptitudes through attempting the practices beneath. Simply do them for no particular reason and see what occurs.

A. Take a stroll through your neighborhood or in nature and make a promise to avoid your head and tune in to things outside of yourself. Contingent upon where you are, this could be feathered creatures, children, traffic or hardware. It could be the hints of waves breaking or leaves stirring in the breeze. Tune in for any amazements. At the point when you discover yourself thinking, serenely note how far you've strolled and afterward return to tuning in to sounds. (It might just be 5 feet, yet that is OK!)

B. At the point when you won't be interfered with, tune in to a bit of instrumental music you have never heard. Possibly discover a few

sites that are great assets for the sort of music you appreciate. Unwind, close your eyes, and truly tune in. Would you be able to make out the different instruments? Are there rhythms that change or rehash? At the point when you discover your mind pondering, take a loosening up breath and take yourself back to the music.

C. In the event that you get diverted or aggravated by sounds, attempt another methodology. Now and then, take a couple of moments to go to them intentionally with interest. Try not to mark them as fortunate or unfortunate; simply keep your ears open. Make an effort not to distinguish what you hear, for example, "the radiator" or "the clock." Attempt to tune in as though you have never heard anything like it and have no clue what it is. Sounds that were bothering may change into something intriguing, melodic, or entertaining with this sort of approach. If you can work on remaining mindful of what you hear without dissecting, judging, or giving your own considerations a chance to interrupt, you might have the option to move this aptitude to a discussion.

CHAPTER - 12

DOES ADHD AFFECT A KID'S IQ?

A favorite truth is that all kids with attention deficit hyperactivity disorder (ADHD) are obviously smarter and also have a greater IQ than children without ADHD. But, there's not any correlation between this illness and intellect.

ADHD impacts individuals in precisely the exact same fashion across large, moderate, and low IQ score ranges.

ADHD is a neurodevelopmental condition that could make it hard for folks to concentrate and to restrain impulsive behaviors. The signs of ADHD in young children are inclined to be familiar, and also a health care practitioner can usually make a diagnosis.

There aren't any supported connections between ADHD and intellect. But some people today continue to compete for this.

ADHD can impact a person's capacity to function at work or in college. This will make it rather tough for them to finish certain regular activities, which may cause different people to feel that individuals with ADHD have lower IQs.

On the other hand, a person with ADHD can also encounter hyper-focus. This symptom is the condition of fixation on something which interests someone. By way of instance, they might show an intense focus on jobs they like doing. This might lead them to seem more competent at a particular school or employment tasks, and it might lead some individuals to think they have a greater IQ.

Another research analyzed cognitive impairment differences between individuals with high IQs who failed or didn't have ADHD. It found that individuals with high IQs and ADHD were more likely to get diminished cognitive function.

Another possible reason that a lot of men and women think in a correlation between IQ and ADHD is your identification procedure. A psychologist or other health care professional investigations ADHD based on long—term

monitoring of potential symptoms.

There's no single test that decides whether an individual has ADHD.

From that long-term monitoring, it might seem as if the individual includes a higher-than-average IQ since they concentrate on their college work. Similarly, it might seem they have a lower-than-average IQ since they find it challenging to concentrate on college work.

It's also possible for health care professionals to misdiagnose ADHD. As an instance, those that are highly working about the autism spectrum, even people with specific learning disabilities, and people with bipolar disease can display symptoms much like those of ADHD.

Reasons

There's no single reason for ADHD scientists are still exploring many suspected triggers. But some of the possible causes of ADHD include:

- Neurobiological states, which an individual's immediate environment can activate

- Genetics

- Vulnerability to particular poisons

- Head trauma

- Early birth

- Diminished amounts of activity in the brain regions that control attention and action

- Vulnerability to cigarette or alcohol while in the uterus

There's no proof to indicate that these variables bring about ADHD:

- Compounds

- Allergies

- Ingesting an excessive amount of sugar

- Consuming foods additives

When a parent you are requesting, does ADHD affect a child's IQ, and then, believe me, you're definitely not the sole one. In the end, should you a little number of internet research, before long, you'll see that ADHD is a psychological illness.

Some sites favor to call it a hearing impairment, or possibly a neurobehavioral disease. No matter

the expression is employed, we're still viewing it as some type of mind-related difficulty, and consequently, we frequently presume it will automatically influence an individual's IQ.

To put the document straight, allow me to guarantee you, ADHD won't and doesn't lead to a diminished IQ. In case you still have your doubts, then simply consider some very famous people, like Albert Einstein, for instance, as well as alexander graham bell, who, like most of us know, changed the world forever.

In short, ADHD isn't likely to decrease a child's IQ, but a kid's IQ does seem to be powerful in the total behavior of kids with this disease. By way of instance, as shown by quite a few research, large IQ ADHD children are more likely to neglect their grades compared to ADHD children with an average or below-average IQ.

ADHD children having an above-average IQ are more inclined to exhibit behavioral misconduct that's severe enough to justify intervention. To put it differently, their behavior can be less suitable than ADHD children with a typical IQ.

To sum up, most research will imply that ADHD doesn't influence IQ, but it does and can affect the capacity to make the most of an above-average IQ.

On a marginally different notice, the total severity of ADHD could be significantly affected by the individuals that are in continuous contact with the ADHD kid. By way of instance, the illness frequently seems to be more difficult in children who grow up in households where there is domestic violence.

National instability also appears to produce the condition worse. Again, studies have found that foster children are somewhat more likely to be diagnosed with the disease than children growing up in a household. Having said this, these studies also have been inconclusive to some huge extent, with lots of researchers claiming that national living conditions do not result in ADHD or perhaps worsen the illness, but they can trigger quite similar behavioral issues.

If your kid is having difficulty in school, in the home, or on social occasions, you might fret about the potential for suffering from ADHD.

If left untreated, it may negatively influence your child's potential, which impacts school performance, social interactions, wellness, and self-esteem. The fantastic thing is that thanks to recent improvements in ADHD support and treatment, now you can do something about this. ADHD center for health and welfare, we concentrate just on treating and assisting people who have ADHD, so that they could reach their entire potential. Successful therapy doesn't affect your son or daughter is all about offering the very best support, advice, and resources you want to be successful. Utilizing our new strategy and inclusive, we bring together some specialists in treating ADHD, doctors, experts, coaches, and support staff working together with you and your loved ones as part of a thorough remedy to successful outcomes.

While most individuals are conscious of ADHD or add, at times, it may cause unnecessary anxiety or misunderstanding. ADHD center for health and wellness, our objective is to help educate and educate families about add/ADHD, also supply them with strategies to successfully deal with this ailment.

Is add/ADHD?

The ADHD implies that means less attention issues with hyperactivity. Most kids with ADHD showed signs of hyperactivity and inattention, but some show signs of care issues. The default option is occasionally known as a kid who's suffering from issues less concentrate (add). But the ad is a form of ADHD.

What are the indicators of ADHD?

The main signs of ADHD, such as listlessness or hyperactivity-impulsivity which are incompatible with their child's era. However, it is essential to note that in order to have an accurate diagnosis it is essential to perform a thorough medical background and complete neuropsychological tests, as in combination with a health assessment. Neuropsychological tests help to consider the amount of attention as other facets of language by learning them as memory, sensory, and reading skills.

Recently, parents of kids with ADHD often are unaware of the trend factors toward hyperactivity and impulsivity, even though at an early period. It's normal to hyperactive kids

under 7 decades older with ADHD, revealed indications of hyperactive behavior consistent. Mothers of kids with ADHD sometimes feel their infant is remarkably active from the uterus, while some parents frequently describe their kids as picky and hard to control if they were infants.

Sort of ADHD?

In accordance with this diagnostic and statistical manual of mental issues (DSM-IV-TR), there are 3 kinds of issues with hyperactivity less concentrate:

- Much of this delay: commonly referred to as attention deficit disorder or add, this subtype requires the absence of focus and attention and upsetting behavior. Kids for this subtype weren't too busy and didn't interfere with classes; however, they often do not finish their jobs, easily diverted, careless mistakes, and prevent work tasks that require mental alertness as well as constant. And don't bother, the indicators are probably missed. These kids tend to be mistaken for laziness, idle, and recklessness. They represent about 30 percent of individuals with ADHD.

- Some hyperactive-impulsive kind: kids having impulsive and hyperactive, but generally does not have any difficulty concentrating. They represent about 10 percent to 20 percent of people with ADHD.

- Connected sort: this is the most frequently occurring and contains all of the indicators of ADHD like inattention, distractibility hyperactivity, and impulsivity. They reveal roughly 50% to 60 percent of people with ADHD.

Myths and truth about add/ADHD

There is a whole lot of misunderstanding concerning the attention issue with hyperactivity less significant components to think about.

Caution: "ADHD is over recognized"

Truth: Based on some recent analysis, add/ADHD is really under-diagnosed. In an article printed in the journal od that the American academy of child & adolescent psychiatry (journal of American academy of child and adolescent psychiatry), dr. Richard d. Todd, Ph.D., MD, reported that the first results of

the research population of twins indicate that "ADHD is currently under-diagnosed, includes an intricate mechanism of hereditary morbidity and optional."

Myth: "poor parenting is the reason for ADHD."

Truth: ADHD isn't caused by poor parents. But research has shown that ADHD is inherited, which might be the origin of the misconception. Lately, data printed in the annals pediatrics (journal of pediatrics) revealed that kids who have ADHD adults are roughly 25 percent of the chance to develop ADHD. Additionally, there are signs that ADHD continues into adulthood is greater as it hastens at the genetics of youth. Some studies have concluded that the lineage is your origin of the majority of the behaviors presented with characteristics of ADHD in kids.

Caution: "ADHD affects men over women."

Truth: in children, the ratio is to 1, because women are usually under-diagnosed. In adults, roughly precisely the exact same number of women and men seek medical aid for ADHD. In kids, women might have symptoms of ADHD in less obvious ways, like speaking too quickly or

as much.

Myth: "concentrate on video games for hours. He can't have ADHD."

Truth: occasionally, individuals with ADHD tend to concentrate too. In other words, concentrate on something and dismiss the other items about you. This might appear contrary to a lot of parents and people who know a person with ADHD.

ADHD and IQ

There's much debate about whether a person with ADHD mechanically has a higher IQ. There's even more disagreement about exactly what such a correlation implies. Based on the severity of symptoms, ADHD can influence an individual's capacity to work at work and school. Everyday tasks may also be hard. This can give the impression an individual has a diminished IQ, as it really isn't the circumstance.

Mothers who had equally high IQs and ADHD have been found to possess a total less cognitive function in contrast to other participants that had high IQ but not ADHD.

A variety of verbal, memory, and cumulative tests were utilized in the research. 1 trouble for this study, nevertheless, is there were not any other management groups. For example, there weren't any ADHD-only or low-IQ classes as an example.

164

CHAPTER - 13

DOES ADHD EVER GO AWAY?

While growing up, our brains continue to develop, but unless the original oxidative stress is healed, the brain develops in a way to compensate for oxidative stress rather than according to its normal design.

The ADHD brain compensates for oxidative stress rather than develop according to its normal design.

Understanding brain science can be quite complex, but this same concept can be easily understood if we apply it to a broken bone that needs to be healed.

If you have a broken bone in childhood, the bone will automatically grow back because the body is designed to heal itself. But unless the bone is properly "reset," according to the

body's design, it will not grow back straight. By resetting the bone, and providing extra protection from further injury with a cast, it not only grows back, it actually ends up stronger than it was before the break.

Similarly, by recognizing the oxidative stress that causes ADHD and then "resetting" the brain with extra support, while also protecting from future oxidative stress, the brain can grow back according to its natural healthy design. It may even grow back stronger. The extra support necessary to "reset" the brain can be a combination of physical, emotional, mental, sensory, and nutritional support.

By "resetting" the brain, we can heal ADHD.

To begin the process of healing, we must first recognize the symptoms of ADHD. By identifying the many faces and later stages of ADHD, we can then address the cause and eventually heal the condition. Without first recognizing that we have ADHD, we are not motivated to seek out and find the answers to heal our condition.

To make matters worse, without the recognition that ADHD is a physical condition of oxidative

stress in the brain, we tend to have become overly critical of others or ourselves. We continue to misinterpret ADHD symptoms as character defects, neurosis, and/or personal failings.

With this new insight, we can view the symptoms of ADHD in others and ourselves in a more compassionate light. We can react to ADHD as we would react to having a broken leg and needing to walk with crutches for a few months.

ADHD does not have to be a lifelong sentence. It can be healed. For some, this insight means they don't have to take dangerous drugs to medicate the condition. For others, it means they become less defensive about having a "disorder" or "mental condition." They are then free to focus on getting the extra nutrition their brain requires. With this new insight, the door opens to explore natural solutions to heal ADHD

The Many Stages of ADHD

Throughout life, our brain continues to grow and develop. Complex brain changes continue into old age, which reflects our degrees of maturity. At every stage of life, ADHD interferes with our

normal development and the expression of our inner potential for success, happiness, love, and good health.

Let's take a brief overview of the new challenges caused by ADHD at six major stages of brain development and maturity:

- Stage 1. Children experience different degrees of trauma related to learning, behavior, and social challenges. The inability to excel in the classroom or form supportive friendships, can seriously limit one's happiness, self-image, and self-esteem, along with his or her ability to trust.

- Stage 2. Teens experience new social challenges, including isolation, bullying, body image, obesity, and addictions. While violence and video addiction are increasing in boys, girls are experiencing more body image problems and bullying. Boys experience late puberty and girls experience early puberty.

- Stage 3. Young adults experience increasing degrees of depression and anxiety and commonly return home after college to live with their parents. More young men

and women are unwilling to make lasting commitments in intimate relationships. Divorce continues to be high, shorter relationships are the norm and there are now twice as many single people.

- Stage 4. Adults experience an increasing inability to manage stress levels, which in turn leads to dissatisfaction in relationships, overwhelm, exhaustion, and divorce.

- Stage 5. At midlife, aging adults face some version of the "midlife crisis" which includes boredom in relationships, depression based on regret, and/or boredom with work and a longing to quit and retire.

- Stage 6. Elders today experience unprecedented levels of modern diseases that were previously not common, including diabetes, heart disease, cancer, Parkinson's disease, dementia, and Alzheimer's disease.

All of these challenges arise from the same condition that gives rise to ADHD but go unrecognized as such.

The Unrecognized Symptoms of ADHD

As we age, our brain continues to grow and develop through different stages. At each stage, if ADHD is not healed, it continues in new and different ways. The childhood symptoms shift into teenage symptoms and so on. The symptoms of each stage remain to some degree but are overlooked or suppressed as new coping mechanisms emerge.

A coping mechanism is not always a good thing. For example, a young ADHD child may inappropriately express painful emotions. As they become older, a coping mechanism may simply be the repression of their ability to feel emotions.

They no longer inappropriately feel and express painful emotions, but they are also unable to feel and express their positive emotions as well. When asked what they feel, they feel nothing, while layers of repressed feelings and limiting beliefs are hidden deep inside their hearts.

A coping mechanism is not necessarily a good thing.

Let's explore the common coping mechanisms of ADHD that may emerge according to the four temperaments.

1. Coping mechanisms for creative children: At puberty, children with a creative temperament who are hyper-focused on seeking new stimulation may no longer be spaced out, bored, or distracted in the classroom. Instead, they learn to cope by creating a kind of tunnel vision or focus that allows them to excel at one thing but limits their ability to enjoy other interests. With great enthusiasm, they may start new projects, but quickly lose interest, procrastinate, or simply do not follow through. They may create unnecessary drama by waiting until the last minute to finish tasks.

They start new projects, but quickly lose interest, procrastinate, or simply do not follow through.

As adults in relationships, they can be hyper-focused on loving their partner in the beginning but may just as quickly lose interest, moving on to a new partner or a new focus that provides a new challenge. They tend to be hot and cold in their relationships. They do not realize that their lack of commitment in a relationship is a

symptom of ADHD but feel they have just lost that loving feeling and have no idea why.

2. Coping mechanisms for responsible children: A child at puberty with a responsible temperament who is hyper-controlling may stop resisting change, but as a teenager, they may become obsessed with being perfect. They may become high achievers, but never feel good enough. They may also become overly stubborn, rebellious, or defiant.

On the other hand, they may compensate by becoming obedient to the wishes of others or their parents. They may become excessively vulnerable to peer pressure. As adults, they may climb the ladder of success and eventually discover they were climbing up the wrong wall.

They may climb the ladder of success and eventually discover they were climbing up the wrong wall.

In relationships, they are often disappointed and may feel they give more and get less. They are often rejected or criticized for being too judgmental or too controlling. They do not recognize that their need for perfection is

excessive and a symptom of ADHD. They feel misunderstood because they are only trying to make things better.

In some cases, they may cope with these symptoms of ADHD by overeating, over-exercising, or oversleeping. They mistakenly conclude they just like to overeat, oversleep, or over-exercise.

3. Coping mechanisms for bold children: When children with a bold temperament who are hyperactive become teenagers, they may be able to sit still in class, but their minds remain busy, distracted, or bored. They may stop fidgeting, but, in their minds, they are somewhere else. It is hard for them to stay focused on a particular train of thought.

Hyperactive teens or adults may develop the coping mechanism of becoming thrill-seekers to avoid feeling bored with the routine of life. Rather than consider their "dangerous thrill-seeking" as a coping mechanism for ADHD to suppress the feelings of boredom, they conclude, "I just like to do dangerous things."

They become thrill-seekers to avoid feeling

173

bored with the routine of life.

They may be unable to relax and enjoy the moment and mistakenly assume that it is just the way they are. They are always busy moving towards some future goal, but unable to appreciate what they have at the moment. Their minds keep them constantly busy thinking up new things to either worry about or achieve.

4. Coping mechanisms for sensitive children: Children with a sensitive temperament who are hyper-vulnerable may develop the coping mechanism of repressing their need for love and, as a result, resist or reject affection, appreciation, or intimacy.

They may become hardened by life and relationships and become overly self-reliant and independent. They always wear a smile because they are determined not to get hurt by depending on another. They can be very loving and giving but are not good at receiving. In intimate relationships, they are easily disappointed and may become moody, anxious, or depressed.

They become hardened by life and become

overly self-reliant and independent.

As adults, they may become overly caring for others to avoid feeling their own vulnerable feelings. Eventually, the denial of their own needs catches up and they feel alone, resentful, or hurt. Rather than recognizing over-giving as a symptom of ADHD, they may just blame others for not supporting or appreciating them enough.

Understanding Coping Mechanisms

Understanding coping mechanisms help us to question and discover who we truly are. Are we simply coping with an abnormal brain condition or are we expressing our true and authentic self? Coping mechanisms can be so automatic that we just assume they express who we are instead of recognizing that we may have ADHD.

In these examples, the coping mechanisms are automatic reactions, attitudes, or behaviors to avoid feeling the original symptoms of our ADHD. They often feel good because they help us to avoid the discomfort of having symptoms of ADHD.

175

Coping mechanisms help us avoid the discomfort of having symptoms of ADHD.

For example, if procrastination to achieve a goal is uncomfortable, a coping mechanism may be oversleeping or making something else more important and doing that. One may even decide to stay in their comfort zone by giving up their goal altogether.

When ADHD is not recognized, we can easily delude ourselves and become addicted to our coping mechanisms. Even actual drug addictions are coping mechanisms to minimize the symptoms of ADHD

CHAPTER - 14

ADHD SKILLS

Your children with ADHD at school and adults with ADHD at work need more skills than drugs can offer to be both confident to be the most effective, alert, or successful. The enemy of productivity or performance is tension. Relaxation is one of the effective strategies for people with ADHD.

Nevertheless, this is not relaxation that is linked to laziness or long holidays. Alternatively, this is a condition of muscle relaxation paired with sufficient excitation. Concentrated and alert, but comfortable.

Deep breathing can help relieve tension and relax. It can also help people with ADHD to better focus and remember.

Many people receiving ADHD treatment are taking stimulants. Stimulants are vasodilators that help improve the performance of the

brain by opening blood vessels and increasing blood flow and brain oxygen. Stimulants also help increase the development of certain brain neurotransmitters.

Deep breathing can also help to add more oxygen to our bloodstreams and brains, helping to improve the performance of the brain. This is something that athletes know. Martial arts people know this. And everyone affected by ADHD must also know this.

Deep breathing on its own will not eliminate effective stimulant therapy. But deep breathing and relaxing exercises can be an important addition to medications, and pills cannot teach you important skills. These are the qualities necessary to achieve greater self-control.

Take 6 to 10 deep breaths. Through the nose until your lungs feel fulfilled. Keep it for a few seconds, then slowly exhale through your mouth. Enable your shoulders each time you exhale to relax more and more. Breathe deeply and fill your lungs and "belly" with air. Relax your muscles deeper than you do.

Do this easy morning workout when you wake up and again on your way to school or work. Do this after lunch and again at school or at work while coming home. And then another time to relax for the night, just before bed.

Why Are People Sighing?

Because suspicion is a natural form of deep breathing, we are hesitating to reduce our stress levels. Deep respiration will help turn our "fight or flight" system off. ADHD patients, in particular, those with the intentive-hyperactive type, are typically on the edge of the autonomous nervous system, the "fight or flight."

Some studies (Fowles, Affective Disorders Journal, 2003, and others) and common sense and experience suggest that the most "tense" people are often at risk of behavior without auto-control.

Such individuals are particularly at risk of vengeance, behavioral disorder, ' poor control of emotional expression, ' and ' disinhibition. ' In other words, someone with impulsive ADHD, in combination with only high levels of muscle tension, may get into a lot of trouble with

their emotions and behavior. When pressure increases, the autonomous nervous system may startup. Our bodies pump adrenaline, noradrenaline, and cortisol into the bloodstream when this occurs. Heart rate increases; breathing gets faster; the field of vision is diminishing. Blood is diverted to our big muscles so we can fight or run away. In connection with ADHD, we can see that in our kids, teens, or partners, the Hulk starts to emerge. This is when your child gets out of school for the week, or your wife gets burned at work.

Deep breathing, as we said, can help to disable our' fight or fly' system. Those with ADHD are normally "on edge" and are often nearly at the start of the autonomous nervous system, the fight or flight system.

Those who are vulnerable to excessive stress or who have ADHD-type impulsive hyperactivity need to do extensive respiratory exercises daily. Then, if a dangerous position in the school or at work arises and your stress levels rise with your muscular tension, the person who has practiced those skills can start breathing deeply, turn down your autonomous nervous

system, keep the adrenaline away for a while and start relaxing.

Progressive relaxation: In addition to a calming state of deep relaxation, gradual relaxation techniques will give you the skills you need to relax and relieve stress in any situation. Good medication can help reduce depression and stress. Instead of using alcohol or drugs to relieve anxiety and stress, learning and exercising relaxing skills can achieve the same results and are much healthier.

Look up yourself as you read this right now. Take your finger and touch your forehead in the middle (from the point between your eyes and about two centimeters above). Note that place. Remember that place. Is this spot on your forehead relaxed? If not, just take a minute to relax.

You will notice that to relax one point, you have to relax your whole front, and your whole face is actually beginning to relax. Then you start to relax your neck and shoulders. It's going to be good, go ahead and relax.

This is a way of teaching kids with ADHD to relax. Robots to Ragdolls. It is a simple technique for progressive relaxation. Render it a match, "Robots to Ragdolls." Have the kid sleep. Then, ask the child to push his feet, "as close as they can... keep it...

Such individuals are particularly at risk of frustration, behavioral illness, poor management of emotional expression, and disinhibition. This means that people with impulsive ADHD associated with just the highest level of muscle stress can have a lot of emotional issues and behavior. Keep it... hold it... then you can relax your feet, and make them as comfortable as a ragdoll.

Now calm down your feet and render them as smooth as a rag doll. Then, get them to do likewise, with their legs under the knee, then over the knee and their stomach, tighten their stomach muscles by pushing out their stomach and then relaxing like a ragdoll. Then your back. Then the shoulders and chest, then your face.

Then ask them to lay down just like a ragdoll but take a tour of their bodies to see if there are still tense muscles. If so, tighten the muscle

group and relax. Then, let the child understand with knowledge what relaxing it feels like. Combine this with a deep breath so that the child can relax further. Allow the child to stay about five minutes comfortable but alert. The more frequently the child practices this ability, the better the child can relax under stress. It is one of the skills needed to learn autonomy.

Then you have them do the same with your feet, under your knees, and over your knees. Next, for your belly, stretch your abdomen by pushing out your stomach and relaxing as a rag doll, to release tension from your head, your shoulders, and your neck. Then ask them just to lie down.

Self-Control, Managing Impulses, and Making Good Decisions

Impulsive behavior frequently happens in children with ADHD and other behavioral disorders. Impulsivity is identified with following up spontaneously or without thought. Therefore, these children regularly do things like face extra challenges, exclaim things, don't sit tight, and interrupt discussions.

In these cases, impulsiveness might be brought about by a cerebrum-based irregularity. Anyway, some strategies can enable your child to develop self-control to limit impulsivity. The accompanying tips will enable excessively impulsive children to more readily oversee behavior and, in this manner, improve social connections.

Now and again, merely monitoring an issue can diffuse it. At whatever point, your child demonstrations impulsively, carry her attention to it, and help her to all the more likely comprehend why the behavior is an issue at that time. While rectifying your child's impulsive behavior, it's essential to do as such in a quiet and accommodating way so as not to influence self-regard contrarily. Try not to make your child feel like the individual in question is the issue, yet instead, the behavior is the issue and sends the message that it tends to be remedied. Nonetheless, remember that now and again, kids won't have the option to control their impulsivity just by investing more energy—so counsel an expert if you keep on having concerns.

Furnish your child with devices to battle impulsive behavior. For instance, if your child tends to interrupt, request that he place his hand on your arm when he has a comment and sits tight for you to recognize him before talking. If your child is inclined to forceful behavior like hitting or kicking other children, urge her to take the hostility out in different manners like gnawing on a pad or kicking at a ball or bramble. It will fulfill their inclination without causing issues or harming others.

Systems like breath mindfulness and care reflection can help improve motor control. Instruct your child to take a couple of full breaths when they feel their energy or impulsivity building. Figuring out how to respite can go far towards helping your child to diminish impulsive behaviors. Full breaths can likewise assist parents with diminishing their frustration that frequently emerges in response to a child's behavior. So, in all cases, make sure to relax!

Recognize when your child is patient and prize him for positive behavior with acclaim or an extraordinary prize. Children who battle with impulsivity need to act and might be bound to

do so when they comprehend what the favored behavior resembles.

If you speculate your child has impulsivity issues or has just been determined to have ADHD, get in touch with us on the web or locate an inside close to you to study how the Brain Balance Program can help.

The ideal approach to enable your child to figure out how to self-direct is to offer help when he needs it. Here are a few different ways you can do this:

Talk about emotions with your child. For instance, 'Did you toss your toy since you were baffled that it wasn't working? What else might you be able to have done?'

When your child battles with a robust inclination, urge her to name the inclination and what caused it. Hold up until the emotion has passed if that is simpler.

Help your child find fitting approaches to respond to forceful emotions. For instance, show your child to take a break or get adult assistance when he feels overpowered. Make statements like 'We should unwind' and 'I can

support you on the off chance that you like.'

Remember to show restraint. It tends to be extremely difficult for small kids to adapt when they have robust emotions.

CHAPTER - 15

INNER SPACE AND BEING

Maybe you're beginning to see what an impact your inner life has on your outer life? In order to make sense of our world and all the activity available to our awareness, the brain creates perspectives, artificial constructions that provide a fixed point, and the idea of a separate self from which to send and receive perceptions. Speaking for myself, when I am aware of this, I'm usually also aware of the greater world of possibilities and so do not feel constrained or limited by this idea. Pure awareness is still available when I recognize this. But when I am preoccupied or absorbed in the details of the perspective and believe that my own perspective is all there is, it becomes narrow, my perception narrows with my figurative field of vision, and I begin to feel cramped or trapped.

Our human creative property is embedded in the very nature of awareness itself. As a result, the properties of the individual perspective that we occupy supports and nurtures our creation of ever more of those properties in our experience. This happens through tiny, foundational processes that are typically outside of the range of our practical awareness but come to define and describe our experience, also known as our interpretation of life itself. This dynamic is but one part of a complex dynamic referenced in the ancient, hermetic teaching, "As within, so without."

When ADHD symptoms are present and unwanted, it is a clear indication that you, or the sufferer, may be bound by the thinking brain, effectively limiting a fresh flow of pure awareness. A person with ADHD can experience these states as though magnified.

An even more dramatic shift potentially occurs when transitioning from thought bound awareness– or what is a wing of awareness–to allowing the open-hearted wing of awareness to influence or even to dissolve the perspective we once created.

Bringing awareness to the formation of our perspectives, whether in retrospect or as we observe them at the moment, determines the clarity of awareness available to our perception at any time. One trick is bringing lighter emotions forward, which are less dense than the heavier emotions that we associate with negativity. That's one simple way to begin. On its own, just feeling good can be a useful set point to work from.

For example, if I'm standing in a river in fast water where I've never been before, the currents can seem threatening and the slippery rocks are like insidious enemies leading me to danger. This feels ominous, and perhaps as you read that, your body tensed up and your awareness was heightened. On the other hand, I may choose to see the present situation a bit differently. If I am in the same situation, yet not resisting the current–instead of going with it and engaging it fully without making my predicament mean danger–the slippery rocks feel silly and playful, and I can move in and out of currents and depths without feeling threatened. Perhaps I find myself instead surrendering to some— allowing them to help me on my way. You can

say that how you are feeling about the form of reality that surrounds you helps determine your perspective and experience. It is the container where it occurs.

Anyone who perceives profound and practical teaching from the words above might also perceive the teaching that ADD, or its presence in others, offers toward our human experience. Let me explain. As a metaphor, attention can be likened to an aperture through which our life experience unfolds, except that this is no ordinary lens one merely peers through. Attention draws both perceiver and the perceived together into one creative field of balanced perception as the beheld and beholder.

Within this field, this container, if you will, there emerges what each perceiving being considers to be their life. From this perspective, we can glimpse both our divine power and our mortal limitation, the entire spectrum of our own existence, indeed. Viewed in power, free will presents us with an ability to create our own experience by creating and choosing our perceptions. In limitation, free will presents only our choices to act within a fixed perception,

however, it was served, it is simply accepted to be. In the first, you co-create by being consciously aware of creative opportunities. In the latter, you create only interpretation based on thoughts: judgments, reactions, and past perceptions.

Presently, Western medicine understands ADHD as a syndrome, a group of symptoms that occur together, and for which there is no single known cause or cure. As one that struggles with ADD, I can say with compassion and humility that I'm grateful there's no known cure, since to me, ADHD can only be known as a state of being... And I, for one, might take exception to there being a cure for that!

To blend some science and experience, I offer these few observations. Currently, ADD is recognized by distractibility, impulsivity, and a myriad of other related expressions. You can say that these symptoms arise as they contrast with, or challenge, the accepted boundaries of a perspective that was actually formed to contain what is deemed necessary or appropriate.

One insight or tip I suggest is to balance the What Is of one's perception, a person must

intentionally offer equal measures of Open-Hearted awareness. Failing to do so by intention will keep us out of balance and locked in a narrower perspective. This narrowness itself results in some inevitable clashes with the spacious contents of the perceived world.

If there were such a thing as "standard" brain functioning, even my perception of being in dangerous waters where mere objects were staged like enemies may be tempered by other parts of my brain engaging and processing a somewhat less black and white situation.

For many with ADHD, the neurochemicals that engage those supporting parts of the brain shut off, and the same transmitters intensify a smaller area of their brain activity. When this happens within an individual, perhaps he is aware that other options for perception may exist, but they are not apparent through the brain activity that is offered at the moment. The result is this magnifying effect–a fact that I use as a metaphor to describe some aspects of the ADD experience. This can precede the very real perceptions of being stuck in a cycle of negative thought that is interpreted as being

caused or created by negative manifestations.

Someone experiencing ADHD symptoms can learn to begin to recognize them as a type of warning. Response or phenomenon, which informs them they are stuck in thinking. When this occurs, they could use some physical change to invite space, in other words, fresh awareness, to unlock the brain's grip on one set of perceptions.

This is self-awareness practice that is recommended to anyone and proves especially helpful in relationships for another person to employ on themselves first, for example, when ADHD symptoms arise visibly in your spouse. This is a comparable metaphor for the instruction you would see for first putting on the oxygen mask in the event of an emergency on board the airplane, as in secure your own oxygen mask before proceeding to assist others. This focus on self-first allows you to be more present and less vulnerable to an unwanted negative exchange. In turn, your self-leadership models for your spouse (and everyone else) a way of being that is best known by experience rather than description or direction. As within,

so without...

The application of modeling in relationships can seem subtle but can have a profound and lasting impact on you, your partner, and your relationship. It changes any dynamic where the perception of right and wrong, good or bad, or roles in a pecking order are hard to break out of. All of these can create resentments and misunderstandings from both sides, and where these areas manifest problems, they are usually indicators of egos requiring something to be a certain way. Modeling is a genuine expression, and as intended, free of manipulation or expectation of any specific result. The ego does not understand modeling, and its best attempt to emulate it will look like trying to control an outcome rather than empowering the authentic creation of lasting change.

One of the ways that our human ego creeps in is by adjusting only behavior that is already anticipating a certain result. Doing this reflects an already diminished view of possibility and, as such, presents new limitations. Even though our experience may support the small-sights view going forward, ultimately, it disempowers

all that surrounds it, not just the object of its gaze. The compulsion or the need to already know how something will be received, or what the outcome will be, ensures that result as well.

At the core of this desire for control is resistance to trust, or to allow what wants to happen, which obscures the flow of pure awareness when the ego is then triggered to come to the defense of some long-held position or belief. These dynamics can be especially apparent in family relationships, or in long-standing, established marital or partnered relationships. These become an issue particularly when imbalanced, as when gains are perceived in other areas of your life, yet we appear or feel trapped when these older, deeper relationships engage.

Often an opening that permits the breach of just one such resistance point in an older relationship, say one with a parent, will be recognized in such stark contrast to previous thought patterns as to be held as a remarkable breakthrough, which weakens reason's grip on other past resistance points–and the relationship is beheld as transformed. Decades of attempts to cajole or control are released

through simply letting go of already knowing how events will unfold, and allowing each being to be as they are. When you let go of knowing another, of effectively limiting another, you hold them in the highest esteem. The beliefs and expectations that you placed on him or her can begin to fall away.

Like so many other of these facets and dynamics, this is true in all relationships and especially so in relation to a person with ADHD. When even the subtlest perception of resistance or conflict arises for someone whose primary challenge exists in regulating attention, the opportunity for change can actually be lost. This truth is expressed in the adage, energy flows where attention goes, and is also borne out in reverse–attention flows where energy goes.

Once triggered, no matter how reasonable other perspectives may be, at the moment, the person with ADD has difficulty perceiving the interaction as anything other than a conflict. Once that judgment forms, it must dissipate, often slowly, as circumstances and events allow a free flow of awareness to enter perception, eventually.

This perception repair is a form of allowing natural healing that some physicians refer to where the autonomic resources on their own are enough to rebalance and restore health to the body. It will work itself out if we simply allow it the time and space to do so. In the brain or psychic portion of the body, conflict and resistance is manifest through resistant thought and behavior. In turn this can eventually be taken on into other parts of the body where it may manifest as illness or dis-ease. As within

CHAPTER - 16

MANAGING MORALE

Morale is associated with energy, mood, drive, agency, motivation, timing, and quality of life. In the military, morale is related to the will to fight. For us, morale is related to the will to keep working around obstacles until we reach our goals. For people already facing an uphill struggle with ADHD, morals can be the deciding resilience factor.

Morale is associated with will, desire, meaning, confidence, and motivation.

When morale is high, we are more likely to believe in our ability to realize our goals. When morale is low, we might feel like giving up rather than persisting.

Morale is related to how we take care of ourselves as well as how we motivate ourselves. People

with ADHD can be particularly vulnerable to de-moralization. If you have ADHD, you must monitor and protect your morale. When you advocate for and are kind to yourself, you are protecting your morale.

Motivational states are like battery packs supplying the energy we need to move forward toward a goal-directed future. Motivational states provide the energy to overcome obstacles and to delay gratification. People with ADHD.

Have an impaired ability to picture the intended future while simultaneously engaging with boring details in the present. The inability to sustain motivation can drain your batteries and lower your morale.

- You will discover some workarounds for the following morale related obstacles:

- You feel beaten down and demoralized by ADHD

- You aren't used to paying attention to your morale

- You are still troubled by memories of being demoralized in the past

- Chronic stress is bad for your morale
- Keeping your energy up can be difficult when there are many (often boring) steps on the path toward a goal
- You have difficulties staying motivated

You feel beaten down and demoralized by ADHD.

ADHD cannot demoralize you. If you feel demoralized, it is probably due to something you have control over. Below are some possible sources of demoralization to be curious about.

- How you take care of yourself
- How you motivate yourself
- How forgiving you are of yourself
- How you show up as your own friend
- Who you listen to?

ADHD cannot demoralize you.

If you feel demoralized, it is probably due to something you have control over.

You aren't used to paying attention to your

morale.

Here is an exercise to help you monitor your morale.

Directions: Set your intention to notice how you take care of yourself. The questions below can serve as a guide.

- How do you tend to treat yourself when you make mistakes?

- Would you be comfortable treating someone else this way?

- How do you tend to treat yourself when you succeed? EG: Do you give yourself credit where credit is due?

- Do you give yourself as much credit as you do criticism? (What is the ratio)?

How do you tend to treat yourself when you make mistakes?

You are haunted by memories of being demoralized in the past. Send your past self some empathy.

Now that you know something about ADHD, you can make a better sense of the challenges you

faced earlier in your life. This exercise offers you a chance to send your past self some warmth and empathy. You can even boost your morale in a memory. Try this exercise below only if you are comfortable exploring these memories. If you feel you are not ready, please stop.

Think of any ADHD-related incident that occurred when you were young such that, when you remember it, you still feel a little bad about it. Perhaps you felt like giving up after dropping the ball on something, or you were scattered at a time when it was important to be focused. Maybe you were embarrassed about forgetting something important. Someone may have made fun of you for being spacey.

Did you assume that you were irresponsible or lazy, etc.?

Picture your past self in that scene.

Imagine speaking warmly to your past self (privately or out loud).

Start sentences with the phrase, "No wonder..."

EG: "No wonder it is so hard for you to sit still in school. You have ADHD," or, "No wonder you

are so overwhelmed. You try so hard, yet you end up late because you don't know that you have ADHD. "The empathy is in the "No wonder you..."

Now picture how your past self-responds to the warmth and empathy. This memory has been altered.

You get stingy when it comes to giving yourself credit.

Do you tend to discount the importance of small steps that you make? (EG: You withhold giving yourself credit until you have completed your goal.) Workaround

Acknowledge any effort that you make, no matter how small.

Since tiny accomplishments can still involve high degrees of difficulty (especially for the organizationally impaired) it is important that you give yourself credit (where credit is due). This is a resilience factor that is within your control.

Try the experiment below to experience how savoring credit can affect you: 1. Write down

any three things that you expended any energy on today, no matter how small.

1. Look at them one at a time.

2. Take a few breaths as you savor each one.

3. Notice how it feels to allow yourself to savor your efforts.

4. At the end of the day, write down everything you expended any energy on all day (no matter how small). Include anything you might tend to take for granted, like parenting, chores, or going to work. Even contemplating something counts.

5. As you savor this list, notice whether the energy level in your body matches the efforts you expended and acknowledged.

Keeping your energy up can be difficult when there are many (often boring) steps on the path toward a goal.

Have fun!

Protect your morale by making sure you are having fun whenever possible.

Spice up the path with what makes you smile.

Listen to music. Make up a game.

Fun is an essential strategy for sustaining attention.

You have difficulties with self-motivation.

We are better able to maintain higher levels of motivation at the beginning (idea) stage of a project. However, we can easily lose that motivation during the later stages. Motivational styles matter when considering their impact over time.

EG: Negative motivation (stress, harshness, fear), for example, may be effective motivators in the short term but harmful in the long term. It is useful to monitor your motivational style. Once you can monitor it, you can fine-tune it.

Notice how you tend to motivate yourself.

Directions: Try to pay attention to how you motivate yourself (using the question provided below). The goal is to observe, not change. It might be helpful to write the question down and stick it in your pocket as a reminder.

It would be ideal to keep a log.

- Do you motivate yourself with stress?

- Do you encourage yourself?

- Do you acknowledge your progress to yourself?

- Do you tend to play to win or not to lose?

- Do you tend to motivate yourself positively or negatively?

- Do you tend to push or pull yourself toward goals?

- Do you motivate yourself with stress?

Protect your morale by taking charge of keeping yourself motivated. You can do this by building motivation into systems of organization, externalizing big picture goals, and building fun into action plans, for example.

I have come across many people with ADHD caught in a cycle of trying and failing. I remember someone telling me, "You can only hit your head against the wall so many times before you give up." This is what it means to be demoralized. The problem is that the majority of these people assumed that they were demoralized because

they had ADHD.

Demoralization is not a symptom of ADHD! It is more likely the result of doing what doesn't work over and over again. Ultimately your morale will suffer if you are expecting yourself to get over your ADHD and function like a normal person. Your morale will be enhanced each time you work around your ADHD.

Finding ADHD-friendly

Pathways to Action

Pathways to action are how you get to your goal. These means involve methods, strategies, and systems of organization. "To dos" are pathways to action. Even If your goal is to enjoy a relaxing vacation in Hawaii you will still have to manage lots of details before you can unpack your flip-flops.

People with ADHD need specialized pathways. You may be failing to reach your goals because you are attempting to follow the same pathways that normal people use without modifying them to make them ADHD-friendly.

Pathways can become slippery slopes

A common error made by people with ADHD is to take on too much at once

You can set yourself up for failure by following ADHD-unfriendly pathways to action

Your brain is organizationally challenged

To-do lists can be very useful. They can also become oppressive and de-motivational

Your mind is susceptible to being organized by the external environment

Pathways to action can turn into slippery slopes.

It is risky to follow a pathway to action without determining whether or not it is ADHD-friendly. Pathways to action are fraught with challenges for people with ADHD. We are at risk of becoming mired in the details involved with the pathway such that we lose track of the destination.

Make sure that pathways to action are ADHD-friendly or can be modified to become ADHD-friendly.

Finding ADHD-friendly Pathways to Action

Obstacle.

A common error made by people with ADHD is to take on too much at once.

Try to bite off less than you can chew.

See if you can do less than you think you are capable of. This may be harder than you think.

Try to bite off less than you can chew.

You are more likely to fail when following pathways designed for normal people.

You may be setting yourself up for failure by relying on ADHD-unfriendly pathways.

For example, normal people can innately estimate the amount of time it will take to get ready for something. People with ADHD who rely on their innate ability to know how much time it will take to get ready for something are probably going to be late and/or unprepared.

CHAPTER - 17

GUIDE FOR PARENTS TO TREAT ATTENTION DEFICIT HYPERACTIVITY DISORDER

Many parents are delighted to learn that treating attention deficit hyperactivity with drugs is not the only option for their children. Although the drugs can help suppress the symptoms of ADHD in some children, they do not work at all in others, and many children simply cannot tolerate the numerous side effects. You will learn more about these side effects and some healthy alternatives that work just as effectively as medications.

Standard medical treatment for ADHD has long been as stimulating as Ritalin. Since children have a so-called "paradoxical system," the administration of a stimulant has an opposite effect compared to that of adults. Instead

of cheering up the kids, Ritalin slows them down. The problem with drugs is that they are not effective for everyone; they have been associated with recreational drug use later in life and have side effects.

With a long list of side effects such as heart problems, stomach problems, insomnia, loss of appetite, and even psychosis, parents have the right to be concerned. Fortunately, the treatment of pharmaceutical attention deficit hyperactivity is not the only option available.

What many parents discover is that natural treatment can be as effective at suppressing symptoms as it is at medications. In the true sense of the word, natural remedies are more effective because they have no side effects. Better yet, they work better than medications because they do much more than suppress symptoms: they heal the brain and restore normal functioning so that your child's brain works optimally over time.

Attention Deficit Hyperactivity Treatment— What to Look for In A Supplement

While there are many natural treatments, some are more effective than others. First, you want to make sure that the supplement contains standardized ingredients that ensure that each dose contains the same combination of medicines with the same dosages. Next, it is important to make sure that the FDA has approved it for safety reasons. Also, here is a list of ingredients that have proven effective:

- Hyoscyamus

- Tuberculinum

- Arsen iod

- Verta alb

Even though you've probably never heard of these ingredients, they have been shown to reduce restlessness, the need for constant stimuli, breakouts, agitation, and hyperactive behavior, as well as calming the nerves and restoring a feeling of serenity and concentration. Since these ingredients have no side effects, a natural attention deficit hyperactivity treatment

can be used with medications. However, it is always best to consult your doctor first.

Conclusion: parents around the world are learning that natural remedies are proven treatments that work better than medications because they not only suppress symptoms but have no side effects or addiction problems. More importantly, they are working to heal the brain and restore function by giving it the nutrients it needs. A word of warning: since the quality of food supplements may vary by manufacturer, and you should do your research to choose the best quality for your baby.

Natural Herbal Treatments For ADHD

Consideration deficiency hyperactivity issue (ADHD) can influence the two kids and adults. Normal ADHD occurs in early childhood, such as hyperactivity, distraction, restlessness, impulsivity, and poor concentration. Although it is diagnosed more and more often, there are some circumstances in which children have mild symptoms and are not diagnosed. These symptoms can occur more frequently in adulthood when life becomes more chaotic, and there are more requests. In the past, ADHD

symptoms were not treated as a disorder, but children were referred to as dreamers, slackers, lazy or troublemakers. Typical treatment for ADHD includes prescription drugs and family therapy to help understand and treat the disorder. Clinical remedies, for example, Ritalin, Concerta, and Adderall, albeit demonstrated safe, have had addictive and mental change impacts in youngsters that made guardians keep away from clinical treatment. Regular medicines are more secure, progressively successful, and increasingly solid to mitigate the manifestations of ADHD. Here are some common natural medicines that guardians can go to while treating their kids with ADHD.

1. Ginkgo Biloba —Ginkgo has been used for thousands of years. Ginkgo has helped treat Alzheimer's, anxiety, depression, ADD, cancer, cataracts, glaucoma, diabetes, impotence, heart attack, stroke, and tinnitus. It stimulates circulation and the nervous system and promotes brain activity. In patients with ADHD, it reduces tissue degeneration in the brain and central nervous system and slows down mental degeneration. Ginkgo increases and optimizes concentration and attention. By increasing

cerebral blood flow, people with ADHD can calm their thoughts and think clearly. As an anti-inflammatory, ginkgo can reduce blood vessel spasms and blood viscosity. This also helps in patients with allergies, asthma, and bronchitis. In large doses, this herb can cause headaches, nausea, and dizziness. However, as prescribed, it is safe for long-term use.

2. Skull Cap—Skull Cap is a relaxing herb that calms and calms the nerves and nervous system without having a calming effect on the body. Slows down the chaotic process and calms nerves in the brain. Strengthens the nervous system so that you can control the thought process and focus on the tasks. Skullcap can also be used to relieve anxiety, a symptom that usually coincides with ADHD. This herb has been utilized to treat coronary illness, disease, anxiety, strain, cerebral pain, sleep deprivation, weakness, despair, and help with discomfort. As a mitigating, the skullcap can improve assimilation, which is viewed as one of the nourishing insufficiencies that cause ADHD and animate liver capacity. Skullcap is accessible in numerous structures and can be made into a tea by including 1 ounce of dry herb to 1 liter of

water or one teaspoon to 1 cup of water.

3. Chamomile—Chamomile has been utilized restoratively as an unwinding, quieting, and relieving herb. Chamomile is perhaps the most secure herb available today that advances are unwinding. Chamomile has many recuperating properties and is an antispasmodic, anxiety, histamine, anti-inflammatory, and antioxidant.

4. Gotu Kola—Gotu Kola is considered to be a regenerating herb, which implies that it expands the body's protection from stress, injury, uneasiness, and weariness. It additionally invigorates body capacities, for example, skin fix, fortifies hair, nails, and connective tissue, assists with fixation and memory. Gotu Kola is a memory and psychological improvement that helps increment persistent mindfulness and information maintenance. As an antibacterial, antiviral, and mitigating operator, it improves bloodstream all through the body. This herb ought to be kept away from if pregnant or breastfeeding.

5. Avena Sativa (Oats) — Although oats are normally used as a food source for humans and animals, they are rich in minerals and anti-

inflammatory and have numerous benefits for the body. Oats can restore and nourish the nervous and integumental systems. Balances sugar levels, helps with eczema, relieves mild depression, and relieves nervous exhaustion and weakness. Oats can be transformed into infusions that can be applied topically to the skin or added to bathwater to soothe inflamed skin. Oats strengthen the nervous system and make patients better able to cope with daily stress.

6. Rooibos-Rooibos is a plant that is grown in South Africa and belongs to the legume family. It is plentiful in cancer prevention agents, minerals, nutrient C, and alpha hydroxy acids. Rooibos goes about as an antiviral, anticonvulsant against uneasiness and hypersensitivities. Rooibos can relieve nervous tension, allergies, and digestive problems. It soothes the digestive tract and soothes skin allergies, such as eczema and induces healthy sleep. Avoid using this plant if you are iron deficient. It is known to influence iron absorption in the body.

7. Lemon balm—Lemon balm is known for its calming and regulatory effects on the body.

Lemon balm can be used to treat anxiety symptoms by lowering high blood pressure, calming palpitations, and reducing rapid breathing. As an antihistamine, it favors skin and respiratory allergies. Lemon balm calms nerves, elevates the mind and dispels sadness. It can also relieve indigestion, nausea and indigestion, relieve migraines, and fight the fever. This herb ought not to be joined with barbiturates as it can build the impacts in the body.

8. Valerian Valerian can be used for anxiety, confusion, migraine, insomnia, depression, palpitations, hypertension, and nervous indigestion. It acts as a sedative on the nervous system, restoring and calming the nerves and the heart. Calms restlessness, stress, and anxiety. Valerian is safe for general use, but high doses can cause hyperactivity and dizziness. Valerian should not be used in children under the age of 12 or pregnant or lactating women. Do not mix with alcohol, prescription sedatives, or antidepressants.

Attention Deficit Hyperactivity Disorder or ADHD—Still Mysterious

ADHD influences a huge number of youngsters and grown-ups in the United States and around the globe. The disorder consists of three subtypes:

1. Mainly hyperactive/impulsive

The child who has been diagnosed with this ADHD subtype shows both symptoms of hyperactivity and impulsivity. They usually have no problems when it comes to attention. The child who has been diagnosed with hyperactive/impulsive ADHD is always on the move, fidgeting and moving, talking endlessly, and getting along with less sleep than their peers, which pushes parents, siblings, teachers, friends, and others to get distracted, as they age. Mature, they learn to compensate for the symptoms and impairments of this subtype. You can try to keep yourself as busy and amused as possible to stay busy. When it comes to impulsivity associated with the subtype, the ADHD child does not control his reactions.

This means that they act before considering the consequences of their behavior and comments. They are attracted to activities that promise immediate satisfaction rather than delayed satisfaction. Children in this category are often classified as unruly, unruly, and mischievous. On the other hand, not all children with severe behavior have Attention Deficit Hyperactivity Disorder or ADHD.

2. Mostly inattentive

Children in this ADHD subtype have difficulty maintaining concentration and focusing on a specific task or activity. Fight boredom all the time. However, when they are busy with something, they find pleasant or inspiring, they can stay focused. This means that they will have difficulties if they have to consciously choose to pay attention to something. It does not mean that they are stupid or slow, nor that they simply refuse to concentrate. It is critical to get that while the ADHD kid realizes very well what is anticipated from him, he is essentially not ready to control his conduct.

Unfortunately, children in this category are often considered to be lazy.

CHAPTER - 18

EMOTIONAL DEVELOPMENT IN CHILDREN

For children, the biggest problem is the influence of family and people at their schools who can easily make a happy go lucky child into one that has no idea about the realities of life. The smallest put-downs to children will affect them immediately as well as continual abuse through either verbal attacks or physical abuse. Each attack will lower the self-esteem of your child or the children around you, which will mean that eventually, they will have to go through some kind of counseling to help them feel good about themselves and be able to cope with life. Since the beginning of childhood, the child's mind is very impressionable and needs to be nurtured and cared for. If you want your child to feel happy and safe in life, then praise and compliments are the best way to go as well as choosing alternative punishments for

naughty children such as time outs or denying them dessert. We would all like to think that we have helped our child develop as best they can, so in doing this easiest path is to walk away when you are angry and then deal with the child once you have calmed yourself down.

From the age of 2 onward, the child begins to test himself or herself and the boundaries that the world has put before them. This is a standard childlike behavior, which is a good way to start the process of emotional development. Not all emotional development is done through interaction and children should be left to discover things on their own from time to time. Problem-solving then becomes a strong part of their day to day life where for children, every first attempt at routine or duty is a problem-solving challenge. Positive reinforcement is encouraged for both good results and poor results and will encourage the child to persist in problem-solving. Tantrums are a way of the child expressing themselves because words often fail them or for those more developed in speech, they feel that words are not adequate to get the message across. Again, positive reinforcement, although at this stage is hard

for a parent is considered the best way to counter-attack the situation. If the child can be persuaded to talk about or signal the problem, then emotional development has worked and the child will be less likely to tantrum again.

The impulse is another problem for small children and even teenagers that have not developed their social interaction skills have trouble with impulsive decisions. Parents need to implement boundaries that control impulsive behavior such as destruction, swearing or even stealing. These attributes are not socially acceptable and will cause trouble later in life if guidelines are not enforced. Emotional development is a spark subject that affects many parts of day to day life beginning at an early age and continues for the rest of our lives. Even the elderly can be subjected to persuasion if they let themselves be manipulated so emotional development should be continuously worked on and emphasized.

Many people seem to not be aware of this aspect, but children's development includes both social and emotional development. Since their birth, until they become adults, children

constantly learn and use the world and its elements to form their personalities. Although we cannot say that there is a huge difference, when it comes to its importance, between the development of a child from the physical point of view and the emotional one, many parents make the mistake to only focus on the first one, and ignore the aspects that can be linked to the second one, mostly because of their lack of knowledge on this area. Anyway, another important aspect that parents should be aware of when it comes to physical and emotional development is that all children are going to evolve in their own unique way.

For example, parents need to know that for their emotional development, crying is a normal thing at babies. Babies try to adapt to the world and they need to see smiles, they need to be cuddled and when they start to recognize the people around them, at about two to three months, they start smiling back. For the emotional development of a baby, it is very important to see parents smiling at them. At about four to six months, babies are able to recognize people and this is why they become more agitated when there are strangers near

them. They can be easily calmed down when they are picked up and they usually start laughing and smiling when they feel safe. Parents should know that such behavior is normal for a baby's emotional development. After 12 months, babies begin showing negative emotions and they start refusing some things. The social and emotional development of your baby is a very normal one if he starts refusing to eat some foods. If the child cries when seeing the closest person, such as the mother, leaving, you should not imagine that there is something wrong with the baby.

The emotional development of a child in early childhood is going to be a normal one if the baby starts expressing feelings of sadness and fear, starting with the age of one. At two years, a child is going to pretty much show his personality. He can be really selfish, so if the kid refuses to share something with a sibling, that fact is a very normal one in his emotional development. The kid will become more independent in time, and this aspect will only evolve as the emotional development of the child is completed. Being aware of these principles of emotional development in early

childhood is very important and parents should not ignore them, to make sure that they will help their children form their own personalities.

Stages of Emotional Development in Early Years

Many people think that emotional development is the ability to go through a wide range of emotions such as anger, pity, and joy; however, there are more objectives to this kind of development. The overall development of emotions also has to do with controlling these emotions and putting them to good use for a favorable outcome. Children do not know about the grieving process because the words involved with death are a new concept to them. When parents split up and get divorced, the children know that there is a difficult time going on, but they are unaware that their feelings of sadness are coming from this development. Tiny children have very little emotional development because their minds have not yet completely developed properly so often you will find that the smaller children age 2 and 3 years old miss out on what is happening around them which is sometimes said to be better than children

aged 4 to 8 years that know what is happening but have no control over how they feel about any particular situation.

By getting involved with your children and helping to explain what is happening in a positive and simplistic way, you can help them get through their early stages of emotional development, especially when difficult times are happening around the children. It is during these times that you must be aware that everything the child inputs from you and outside sources will influence their ability to develop more emotional range in the future. By using a variety of resources, you can help to develop the children's positive aspects to life no matter how difficult their journey through life starts out. By developing their emotions early, you will be able to help the children later in life where they will be able to make more informed decisions about what is happening around them.

CHAPTER - 19

MOOD FOODS: HOLISTIC
EATING FOR MANAGING ADHD

Recent studies by Yunus (2019) from the renowned Exceptional Parent have asserted how there is a possible link between ADHD and high sugar, salt, and fat intake when kids receive diets with only minimal whole grains, fruits, and vegetable intakes (p. 24). Many findings specifically herald the benefits of a whole-food plant-based (WFPB) diet with minimal or no processing for protection against ADHD, cancers, heart disease, osteoporosis, and other chronic conditions (Yunus, 2019, p. 24) as well.

While I am not suggesting a rigid Biggest Loser style diet or any particular dietary model, I want to offer some general mood foods and natural drinks that not only taste great but are healthier options for you and your kiddos as far as mindful eating. I also want to arm you with

research and resources, so you can explore and take it to the next level as far as what is best for your particular family's needs.

Are you ready for some yummy suggestions? Let us find those aprons, ok?

- Snack Attacks: Make snack attacks healthy with fresh fruits and veggies. Make healthy smoothies together and add some chia and flax seeds to balance moods. Masterchef Junior, anyone?

- Mr. and Ms. Clean: This advice does not mean operating a pristine household free of dust bunnies and flawlessness, but it is about eating as clean as possible to avoid unnecessary additives and food colorings. Of course, kids are attracted to the colorful, marshmallow, vibrant products that are often so full of crap. Yunus (2019) also divulges how we have a clear responsibility as parents and the ones who typically purchase the food products to ensure that nutrition is clean for children, tweens, and teens with ADHD since "This is a controversial subject and, because we often have an emotional attachment to food, we are reluctant to look at this as an

adjunct treatment" (p. 25).

- Diggity D: There is "No Diggity" about it that Vitamin D is the superior sunlight vitamin that most kids, tweens, and teens often lack from excessive indoor gadget time, nutritional voids, etc. As a result, Laliberte's (2010) "Problem Solved: Winter Blues" from Prevention insists that we must all ensure that our family members are digging it with vitamin D proactively since it is closely linked to keeping our serotonin levels elevated and balanced (p. 48). This connection is something super important in kids, tweens, and teens with ADHD for critical brain balance and overall wellness.

- Are you excited to dig it with D? Take a family hike, jog, stroll, or skate around the block. Find a local park and dive into the D!

- Straight from the Hive: Try warm milk with Manuka honey for a natural relaxer before bedtime with your kiddos. My girls really love it on bananas with peanut butter and chia seeds, too. You can also add it to evening herbal teas to evoke some sweet dreams and deeper sleep.

- As a slight disclaimer, because of honey's sugary contents, be sure to just use a small amount, roughly the size of a poker chip. Just do not try to karaoke Lady Gaga's "Poker Face" song, or you might lose face with older kids! BEE holistic, BEE well, and BEE wonderful when you try honey with your honey!

- Sugar High: As adults, we really need to embrace the "You are what you eat" mindset with all kids, but especially those who have ADHD. In turn, closely monitor sugar intake with their candies, sodas, caffeinated beverages, and all those ooey-gooey treats and desserts. Carefully monitor the amount of fast foods that you are serving to your families, no matter how tempting or timesaving it may seem. Studies encourage us to eat "clean" as clean as possible as opposed to relying on fatty, greasy, overprocessed foods. Clean eating will naturally "eliminate unnecessary food additives such as artificial colors, flavors, sweeteners, and preservatives that do not add nutritional value and may contribute to ADHD symptoms. Limit sugar intake to 10% of total calories daily (roughly 6 teaspoons for children aged 2 to 19 years)" (Rucklidge,

Taylor, & Johnstone, 2018, p. 16).

My own daughters recently attended a birthday party with tons of sugary cakes, candies, and fruity drinks. They then began bitterly bickering in the car on the ride home to no avail from all the junk in the trunk (literally). Are you eager to crush that sugary rush and move toward mindful eating? I have been baking and cooking with dates as a natural sugar alternative when I make muffins and other goodies lately. While I am not a professional cook or baker by any means, I encourage you to freely consult cookbooks at the local library or online that focus on mindful and natural ingredients to curb those high sugar sensations that tend to exacerbate ADHD! Be mindful when dining out and always looks for healthier family options.

Putting a freeze on fast food addictions can be so instrumental. La Valle's (1998) pioneering article from Drug Store News also indicates how high sugar intakes can cause low blood sugar and chromium depletion. The fast-food frenzy is really taking a toll on our kids as "The average American now consumes an average of 152.5 pounds of sugar in a year. That large soft drink

at the drive-through window contains roughly 22 to 27 teaspoonfuls of sugar. It is reported that increased sugar intake actually increases urinary chromium excretion. Over time, this could have an impact on behavior" (CP13).

- Move Over: Dairy overload can often cause major digestive issues. When kids are literally plugged up, they can act out even more. To counter these tummy troubles, consider some new dairy alternatives like almond, soy, coconut, cashew, and oat milk. I also suggest adding probiotics to your kiddos' diets with more kefir, Greek yogurt, and other mood foods. In my daughters' cases, they have been extremely helpful to tame tummies and boost moods. Let us Move over mindfully!

- Veg Heads: You can opt for a Meatless Monday approach for more mindful family eating. Try to replace traditional noodles with veggies such as asparagus, zucchini, carrots, etc. Indulge in Brussel sprouts, cauliflower pizza crust, corns, asparagus, etc. Be a vicious veg head and also add more veggies to morning egg dishes, especially omelets.

Make the Jolly Green Giant proud and be a

veg head of household more often to facilitate holistic health and happiness in all kids, but especially ones with ADHD! My oldest daughter adores making and eating kale chips with me. She has also recently been trying the freeze-dried snap peas, too. We never know what they will like until we experiment, right? Go beyond broccoli and green beans on your next grocery run!

In essence, it is also highly advantageous to ensure that your kids, tweens, and teens are getting enough B vitamins in their diets: B1 is linked closely to many key functions like immunity, heart support, and mental processing; B2 offers energy, hair, skin, and eye health; B 3 stabilizes our memories, moods, and hearts; B5 can keep cholesterol levels in check; B6 is a sleep reliever. Are you ready for some "Sweet Dreams" by Queen Bey?

Finally, buzz with B-12 for increased mood and energy management. My young kids love the "classic ants on a log" snack with peanut butter, cashew butter, sunflower seed butter, or almond butter slathered onto celery with raisins, dried cherries, or cranberries. Have fun

in the kitchen and make Rachael Ray proud in a healthy and mindful way today!

- Beanie: While I am not talking about the cool, fashionable hats, try to eat more mindfully against ADHD with beans and legumes. Make black beans burritos, hummus with chick-peas, serve up some edamame, and add lentils or sunflower seeds to beam up your families' diets!

- Magnesium Magnets: Strive to add more magnesium into your family's overall dietary routines, especially in cases of ADHD. Studies describe how the average American is often highly deficient in magnesium "by about 70 mg daily. Magnesium is the calming mineral since it is the principal mineral used to control the parasympathetic nervous system. There is also the potential for calcium deficiency. Many children complain of aching legs and will see positive results with the initiation of a well-formulated multiple mineral supplement" (La Valle, 1998, CP13.). Get your magnesium magnets via food or supplements today!

- Finding Nemo: Set a goal to serve a fatty fish

to ramp up those Omegas and vitamin D 2-3 times a week. Yunus (2019) reminds us of compelling research that depicts how those with ADHD may also have "lower levels of omega-3 fatty acids and higher levels of omega-6 that may lead to inflammation and oxidative stress."

Accordingly, Evidence by Rucklidge, Taylor, & Johnstone, (2018) also suggests that supplementation with omega-3s and/or a broad spectrum of micronutrients (for those not taking medication) may be beneficial for ADHD symptom reduction, but it is so important that all "Patients should consult with their primary care provider before starting any supplement and with a dietician before changing their diet" (p. 15). Get your rod and reel in some fishing action during family meals and snacks for more mindful eating.

In fact, salmon nuggets and fish sticks are always major hits with my girls! They also enjoy coconut shrimp with fun and tasty dipping sauces. How can you get your Nemo and Dory on and blast more fish in your weekly menus?

See for Yourself: Fruits like pineapples,

grapefruits, tomatoes, berries, mangoes, oranges, and kiwis, are a definite self-care saver for the blasts of vitamin C. I also recently discovered passion fruit, a rich source of beta-carotene and vitamin C, as recommended by the recent article aptly called "Mood Food" (2019) from Daily Mail.

My girls love to toss some seeds onto their morning yogurt parfaits. Try some today and see for yourself if your kids will likely say "Yay!"

Zing with Zinc: Assist your kids with ADHD in the culinary department to better zing against mood swings, common colds, flus, and other physical problems. Simply add more fruits and vegetables rich in zinc to their diets daily.

Honor the great pumpkin! Don't wait for Halloween and toss some pumpkin seeds to kids' sandwiches, baked goods, cereals, oatmeal, yogurts, pastas, salads, etc. Experts praise them for reducing feelings of anxiety (Mood Food, 2018), something that kids, tweens, and teens with ADHD know all too well, right? Let's zing and sing with zinc!

CHAPTER - 20
MOOD DISORDERS

This information is included so that you can begin to either realize that your child does or does not appear to have a "mood disorder." As you scan these symptoms, think of your child's behavior/emotional patterns. Is there any match or none? Notice I said "any match," because many ADD/ADHD children do have mild mood disorders.

Types

Bipolar I—frequent/marked mood swings; appears as severe irritability in children

Bipolar II—mostly depressed with occasional up-swings

Cyclothymic—milder form of Bipolar I

Bipolar NOS (non-specific)—serious moodiness; but, doesn't fit above

Childhood Symptoms

- Thermoregulatory system—feeling hot or cold

- Family history of Mood Disorders and/or Alcoholism

- Seasonal mood variations—summer up, winter down

- Anger dyscontrol—tantrums with profanity and threats

- Excessive cognitive or motor behaviors—impulsive and compulsive behaviors

- Dysregulation in executive functions—focus, organization, planning, ST memory

- Over reactive stress response—heightened reaction to real or imagined stressors

- Low threshold for frustration—when required to sustain attention/effort, or to wait

- Frequently with multiple comorbid diagnoses—ADHD, OCD, ODD, Anxiety Disorders, Enuresis, etc.

- Marked mood/energy swings—rapid, wide

variations of emotion, levels of arousal, excitability, and motor activity

- Mood cycle acceleration and/or increased aggression—when given anti-depressants, stimulants, steroids

- Low threshold for arousal, high anxiety, irritable mood—easily over-aroused, sleep/ wake cycle disturbances

- Dysregulation in pleasure sensation— wide fluctuations in self-esteem, appetite, addictive behaviors

- Symptoms worsen with age—sharing features of attention, anxiety, and conduct disorders

ADHD and Sensory Processing Disorder

ADHD and Sensory Processing Disorder (SPD) are distinct disorders, but they frequently occur together. So, it is extremely important to be aware of SPD.

Different treatment approaches apply to each; thus, it is also important to be able to distinguish one from the other.

SPD means that the individual has one or more difficulties in the way(s) in which their brain "processes" information within the six sensory areas (explained in more detail below). Yes, it is a brain-based disorder, too.

Prior to 10 years ago, there was very little awareness of Sensory Processing Disorder (SPD) in the mental health field; indeed, within any professional field except occupational therapy. In the past 15 years, the occupational therapy field has done significant research as well as advocacy to spread awareness of SPD.

Here are some ways to distinguish ADHD from SPD:

- Attention difficulties are greater in ADHD vs. SPD.

- More physical complaints, anxiety, depression.

- More difficulty adapting.

- ADHD+SPD more sensory problems than only ADHD.

- ADHD+SPD more attention difficulties only SPD.

- SPD react more to sensory stimuli (auditory, visual, movement).

- Those with just ADHD do not display this reactivity.

What's most important here?

Once again, treatment must be tailored to the specific child's symptoms. ADHD typically benefits from medication plus behavioral therapies focusing on strategies to improve attention, hyperactivity and/or impulsivity. Children with SPD benefit more from sensory-based occupational therapy designed to enhance their ability to modulate behavior in response to their sensory environment.

More About Sensory Processing Disorder

Sensory processing problems not only frequently occur along with ADHD, but they are a common characteristic of autism. So, again, it is important to be able to distinguish. Misdiagnosis happens all too frequently in these areas.

Sensory Processing Disorder (SPD) has several aspects:

- Vestibular Disorder—trouble with balance, body-position

- Proprioceptive Disorder—sense of pressure, pain, motion

- Tactile Disorder—hyper or hypo sensitivity to skin stimuli

- Oral Sensory Disorder—hyper/hyposensitivity in mouth

- Olfactory Disorder—trouble with sense of smell and taste

- Auditory Disorder—trouble processing noise/language

- Modulation Disorder—trouble controlling stimulation level

Sensory Modulation Disorder (SMD) is a category of Sensory Processing Disorder and the most commonly diagnosed form of SPD. When a child has sensory modulation difficulty, they have significant trouble regulating responses to environmental stimuli. They may over-react,

under-react, seek stimulation, or fluctuate among these. In actuality, the child with SMD has difficulty regulating their responses to bodily sensations created by one or more of their sensory systems.

Other categories of SPD include Sensory Discrimination Disorder (difficulty interpreting sensory stimuli) and Sensory Motor Disorders (most common one, handwriting trouble).

Signs of Sensory Modulation Disorder:

Sensory Defensiveness or Over reactivity

- Strong like or dislike certain types of clothing
- Refuses foods because of textures
- Avoids things like swinging or spinning
- Swings incessantly
- Does not like to be touched
- Often rolls themselves up in a blanket
- Strenuously avoids certain sounds

Under-reactive

- Doesn't notice touch or movement
- Often engages in sedentary activities
- Often doesn't notice obvious sights and/or sounds
- Often not responding to social cues

Sensory Seeking

- Loves to run, jump; rough play
- Likes bright lights, loud music
- Puts inedible objects in the mouth (past age 3)
- Delay in toddler speech development
- Excessive talking

Writing Disorders

(People with ADD/ADHD are more likely to have this.)

Roughly 60% of children with ADHD have disorders of written expression.

The problem for some children is weak skills in

identifying language sounds (called phonemic awareness); for others, it is a motor processing (or, physical movement) difficulty. And, then, for others, the problem is a difficulty in organizing thoughts, letting-go of one set of ideas, shifting to another set and re-organizing them; and, then, gathering the energy and attention to complete the task. Anyone of these problems will make writing an overwhelming and frustrating task, one that a child will avoid or actively resist—strongly, and with increasing irritation and anger.

What Happens to this Child Over the Years?

"But, some of these kids are such good talkers!"

Speaking is a more spontaneous act while writing is a purposeful, directed task. Verbally, we can voice our thoughts, talk about and around them, go off into different directions, and come back to some point. Writing goes much more slowly and requires more precision. Writing is a task of drafting, elaborating, re-drafting, revising, and... eventually polishing. For kids who have low frustration tolerance (that's most ADHD kids), this is a prescription for failure. No wonder they often have a very negative reaction

to the demand that they write.

Many of these processes that a child uses in writing are in the realm of "executive functions." Research is increasingly showing that a high number of children with ADHD have deficits in executive functions.

Executive Functions Effect on the Writing Process

Whenever a person approaches a problem or a project, they must use the following executive functions:

- Analyze the problem
- Plan and implement strategies
- Anticipate problems
- Organize strategies (break into parts, set time-lines)
- Monitor progress, assess if the plan is working
- Remain flexible
- Reformulate plan if not working
- Reassess any new strategy

- Follow the adjusted plan through to the finish

- Monitor need for rest, sleep, food during the task

- Monitor ability to continue without these

- Inhibit impulses that might throw this process off-track

- Store thoughts/ideas for instant use/re-use during the task

ADHD kids encounter difficulties in most of these areas! Just think about your child as you review the above list. You can probably picture their negative reactions at each step, right?

Working Memory

Working memory is the ability to hold information in short-term memory while "working" with it toward solving some problem or putting it in some particular order. Most ADHD kids have trouble with writing because they are either unable to keep information in working memory, or because they are not able to recall that information from working memory.

Core Strategies

1. Your Attitude

You must accept the fact that a child/teen with ADD/ADHD has a real neurological (brain-based) impairment.

2. Adult to Adult Unity

If you're not part of the solution, you will become part of the problem! Develop your "self-care" skills and "team" coordination skills. If you're "stressed-out," "frustrated-to-the-max," or feeling all alone, you're not going to do very well in coping with your ADD/ADHD child no matter what methods you use!

3. The Law of Greater Effectiveness

Simply put—experience and research have identified treatment and management strategies that are proven to be greater in effectiveness. Experience and research have also identified treatments and strategies that are less effective or wholly ineffective.

4. Bottom-Line

There are absolutely no treatments or behavior

management strategies that work every-time, 100% of the time, with every ADD/ADHD child. These just don't exist. So, remember this when some approach seems not to work. Be determined! Stick with it! Re-group. Perhaps re-tool the strategy, but keep going!

Basic Strategies

1. Corral urges for a "Quick fix." Haste makes waste! This will worsen the situation! Think of the last project you handled in-haste.

2. Pick 2 or 3 problem behaviors. No More. State them in clear, brief form. Next to each one briefly describes alternative behaviors you would like them to display.

3. Make this list written. Discuss these expectations with them. Give them a copy. But don't make it a "contract."

4. Give generous Encouragement. Be +!! Powerful tool! Research says that one negative remark can "cancel-out" 6 positive ones. So, save yourself some extra trouble—stick with positive comments.

5. Avoid Over-Reacting. Excessive or frequent

displays of anger or frustration are destructive (hostile, challenging, in-their-face approach). This includes silent pouting.

6. Avoid Negative Reinforcement. It is Disastrous! (Excess criticism, disparaging remarks, efforts to embarrass, numerous/lengthily restrictions, and hitting of any kind!).

They'll give it back 10x.

7. Learn "Active Listening Skills."

A good book: "How to Talk So Kids Will Listen and Listen So Kids Will Talk" (by Faber and Mazlish). Listening is an art. It takes practice. It has a Powerful Effect!

8. Ignore Minor Misbehavior.

Realize That the Majority of Their Misbehavior is "Minor." Pick your battles!

9. Remember:

Your reactions to your child's behavior are a powerful Reinforcer. Whether positive or negative may not matter. Your reaction(s) may Reinforce their behavior, anyway! Many ADHD kids are "stimulation seeking" or

"conflict seeking." Think—which behaviors am I Reinforcing?

Intermediate Strategies

1. Read "All About Attention Deficit Disorder"

by Thomas Phelan. The most down-to-earth, comprehensive book around.

2. Transitions.

Shifting gears, one place to another, one activity to another. They either come "unglued" (get hostile, oppositional, silly) or "freeze-up" (get quiet, withdraw). Anticipate these "events." Make preparations: (1) Tell them about a transition ahead of time; (2) Tell yourself, so you're ready; (3) Tell other family so they can either let you handle it or actively support you; (4) develop strategies for handling each problem transition you've identified.

3. Time-Out.

An extremely valuable tool, only if used properly. Think of it as a way of defusing and/or re-directing. Drop ideas about it being a way to "punish," to "make a point," or to "get them to think about what they did."

Keep it short. Time-outs are much more effective if they are repeated (for repeated misbehavior) rather than increased in length.

4. Use Natural instead of contrived Consequences.

Example: A "Natural" consequence for a school problem would be parent-teacher communication. Contact them by phone or email. Better yet, go to the school with your child to discuss the problem.

CHAPTER - 21

BUILD SELF-ESTEEM

Help children learn about their self-concept. Write at the top of the sheet paper, "Who am I?" and ask students to see how many answers they can give. This forces students to think about their self-concept and gives you an opportunity to explore these ideas in greater detail as well as use insights gained from this activity in your daily interactions with the student.

Reinforce positive behavior, even if it is not a part of the current lesson or activity. Seize every opportunity to reinforce positive behavior. It establishes a pattern of support for good behavior and it builds self-esteem and self-confidence.

Do not offer empty praise or compliments. Self-esteem is easily damaged by uncritical positive feedback. The student quickly learns that they are praised for doing little or nothing

of importance and this signals to them that whatever they do is of no consequence.

Self-esteem is best established by providing the student with tasks that are at the outer limits of their ability, giving them the support and guidance needed to accomplish the task and then praising them for effort and a job well done.

It has become part of our culture to praise children for the effort they put in regardless of the results. We have all seen examples of older students who fail a test or a course or fail to get a job and say sadly, "But I did my best." It can be a harsh lesson that doing your best is not always good enough to claim the reward. Teachers are in the best position to teach this lesson in a supportive benign context.

Students with poor self-esteem usually view their lives as mostly negative. Keeping a journal is a practical way to encourage a child to pay attention to important positive experiences too. Ask students to make brief entries each day, noting their best and worst experiences. They can also record what they did in each circumstance.

Older students can be encouraged to record events they feel strongly about. This assignment encourages more awareness of feelings. These journals are not private diaries and that should be made clear from the beginning. The purpose is to generate discussion about experiences and feelings.

Use a personal timeline. Hold a sheet of paper horizontally and draw a line about a third of the way from the bottom from the left-hand margin to the right. Begin at the left with birth and ask the child to write important events and experiences in her life. You will need to stimulate the students thinking with some examples common to most people. Children, even adolescents, take delight in hearing stories about their childhood, so encourage your students to talk with their parents as they construct their own personal timeline.

The "success a day" program asks students to describe a successful experience each day. Children may initially find the task difficult, especially the negative child who focuses primarily on failure and problems. Moreover, younger children may find this difficult and

describe positive experiences that are not necessarily successful.

Younger students with ADHD will need more direct instruction, role-playing a practice in activities than their peers may learn incidentally. For example, taking turns, the rules of a game, and patience with another player are usually learned in the course of the activity, but for the student with ADHD, we might have to provide special instructions.

Teach friendship and social skills. Some students with ADHD need to be taught specific strategies for joining others in play without being aggressive or unduly provocative. They may need to be taught how to compliment others and how to make requests, so others respond favorably.

Teaching these skills requires time, modeling, rehearsal, review and practice, practice, practice.

Be mindful, that many students with behavior problems are the ones you would like to avoid, especially if they are minding their own business. You may be so grateful that a usually troublesome student is doing his work or just

sitting quietly that you avoid eye contact or any effort to bring him into the conversation. In the short term, this is helpful; in the long turn, it undermines your relationship with that student and sends messages about his own inability to work productively in the classroom.

Attribution theory tells us that students attribute their success or failure to luck, intelligence, skills, how hard they worked, or the difficulty of the task. Students with ADHD, with a history of failure, may blame themselves or they may be more likely to blame others. Feedback, in the form of positive reinforcement, must take all this into account.

Using Rewards, Feedback, and Reinforcement

Feedback should be contingent. That is tied closely in time to the behavior. Reinforcement at the end of the lesson or the end of the day is good but not as powerful for the student with ADHD as reinforcement that comes immediately.

Be specific in your praise or reinforcement. Saying "good" or "You all did well today," is fine, but it is better to tell the student exactly what

they did that merits your prose.

Praise should be appropriate and credible. Empty praise or false praise always backfires in the long run and undermines both your relationship with the student as well as the student's self-esteem.

Offer reinforcement for behaviors that are meaningful. Praise for a tasteful blouse or attractive shoes, might be helpful for the student who made the blouse in sewing class or for the student who struggled to decide on what shoes to buy, but they are otherwise meaningless and, if used as a substitute for behavior or personal characteristics that are more relevant to the classroom, do not further your goals for that student.

Always follow through with rewards and consequences.

Do not say yes just because it is easier at the moment

Not everyone responds to the same reinforces. Whether you are working with a formal behavior modification program with systematic rewards or you are doing rewards informally, be creative

in the way you develop reinforcements.

The best reinforcements are privileges, not things. This is because students will eventually satiate on anything you can choose as a reward that is tangible, but there is an unlimited need for non-tangible reinforcement such as privileges. For example, free time as a reward never gets boring.

Other good refiners include earning lunch with the teacher, using the computer for fun with a friend, leading a game or activity, being allowed to restructure some activity or class schedule. 8. Variable reinforcement produces more resilient behavior. This means that if we want to teach good habits, we are better off reinforcing at different intervals and rates than giving regular reinforcement. It also means that troublesome behavior that is learned with variable rates of reinforcement is harder to change.

Use very simple tangible rewards as often as you can.

The choice of seating is a valuable reward.

Positive comments should outnumber negative comments in the classroom ten to one.

Remember that consequences are logical or natural results of the behavior.

78. Punishment may have no relationship to the behavior, but the rules for punishments should be clearly spelled out in advance.

Often the best reinforcement is a direct outgrowth of the misbehavior. For example, if a child completes seat work or homework three days in a row, the child has earned a credit that can be cashed in for a day; he is excused for homework whenever he wants to use the credit.

You might counsel parents along the same lines. Each night the child goes to bed without protest or sits down to homework without a fuss earns a point. Four or five points can be cashed in to stay up late or avoid homework whenever the child chooses.

You may not be able to come with a large list of reinforces just sitting at your desk, but if you are alert to the wants and needs of your students over a period of time, you will be able to add many items to the reinforcement menu.

Positive reinforcement is always better than taking away something as a behavior modifier. Occasional, it is necessary to deprive a student of some privilege or special opportunity, but that sort of management should be used as little as possible. It is usually possible to set up behavior modification with positive rewards for good behavior rather than punishment for bad behavior.

A reward or reinforcement menu with many different items that cost different prices allows the child to select for an immediate reward if he chooses or save up for a big deferred reward. 193. Typically, positive reinforcement is a better means to change behavior than taking away privileges or the use of other response cost systems. A response cost system is a plan wherein the student begins the hour or the day with a certain number of points or tokens and then loses one for each instance of misbehavior. However, the advantage of the response cost program is that it is more concrete and immediate than some other reward system that requires the child to accumulate points for a reward in the future. Use this type of negative reinforcement as little as possible and use it

cautiously.

Although students with ADHD may need advance notice of a change in routine or direction of activities, do not give more than one warning for misbehavior.

Do not use school-home reports that are limited to smiling faces and negative faces.

Do not use daily reports if it means that the child receives more than 10% negative reports. Frequent negative reports are a signal that the planning in the classroom needs revision; It is not a valuable means to change behavior.

Be explicit in your conversations with parents about the consequences of a negative report from you. Parents often err, making consequences or punishment either too severe or insignificant.

Praise improvement, not just perfection.

Praise often. Set a goal to offer praise at least ten times an hour. This is in addition to reinforcing correct answers with the word, "yes."

Be specific. Label the behavior you like. 29. Divide reinforcement into two parts in your

mind. When first learning a task or behavior, reinforcement should be frequent, immediate, and contingent. That is, it should come right after the behavior and you should make clear what the reinforcement is for. It is fine to tell someone they did well today as you see them out of your classroom door. That can't hurt. But it does not do much good either. It is better to offer the feedback immediately and to explicitly say why you are giving the feedback or reinforcement.

CHAPTER - 22

THE CLASSIC DEFINITION IS MISLEADING

THE CLASSIC DEFINITION of ADHD is found in the Diagnostic and Statistical Manual of Mental Disorders (DSM-5). It breaks down ADHD into 3 types:

ADHD Predominately Inattentive Presentation (often referred to as ADD)

ADHD—Predominately Hyperactive/Impulsive Presentation

ADHD—Combined Presentation (Both Inattentive and Hyperactive/Impulsive Presentations.

The severity of the ADHD symptoms is then defined as severe, moderate, or mild. There is also an option to diagnose the ADHD in partial remission.

These three diagnosis categories have been used for years. Attention Deficit Hyperactivity Disorder is the last of three previous labels assigned to ADHD in the Diagnostic and Statistical Manual of Mental Disorder (DSM). It's hard to believe, but before 1968 ADHD was commonly referred to as "minimal brain dysfunction." In 1968, (DSM-II), it was referred to as Hyperkinetic Reaction of Childhood; in 1980, (DSM-III), it was Attention-Deficit, ADD; and in 1987 (DSM-III-R) it was labeled Attention-Deficit Hyperactivity Disorder. Each of these labels is misleading. Based on the diagnosis name, you may think it's only about being "hyperactive," "impulsive," "inattentive," and nothing more. Truthfully, many normally developing children are at least somewhat hyperactive, impulsive, and/or inattentive. Inattention, hyperactivity, and impulsivity are only a few of the symptoms of ADHD, but there are many more that are described. The diagnosis name itself is due for a change, as it is misleading as to what ADHD really is.

What is Really ADHD?

Keep in mind, the ADHD descriptions and symptoms below are things we all experience to some extent or at some point in our lives. The difference in ADHD children is that these symptoms are (1) constant, (2) regular in all settings (like home and school), and (3) cause significant disruption and impairment in those settings. When the three criteria are observed, a trained professional that specializes in ADHD is recommended to make an official ADHD diagnosis. Here are the typical traits you will find with an ADHD child.

Their minds are not inattentive, but in reality, open and striving to be stimulated. Ideas and thoughts run through their mind at a much higher rate than people without ADHD. Unfortunately, at times this can be overwhelming. Sounds, sensations, and sights can flow into an ADHD child's mind all at once.

Imagine you are at a boring training seminar. While the speaker gives his presentation, there are multiple flashing lights on the right side of the stage, a loud stereo blaring on the left side of the stage, a large HDTV behind the presenter

showing the "20 Most Outrageously Funny Cat Videos of All Time," and somebody behind you continually kicking your chair. Now, what did the presenter say? Welcome to the world of an ADHD child. Kids with ADHD may be overly distracted by noises outside the classroom, a tag on their t-shirt, or people moving around in class. It is as if their brain just will not say "no, I'm not letting you in" and is sucking in all the information at once. They are ultra-focused to everything going on around them. Are they "attention deficit?" If they were more "attention deficit" to all those things going on around them, it would actually help them focus. Kids with ADHD are way too attentive, not "attention deficit."

Being open to a flood of thoughts isn't always a bad thing. Goleman's best-selling 2013 book, FOCUS: The Hidden Driver of Excellence, identifies something called "open wondering" as a characteristic of the ADHD child's brain. They seem to be better able to let go of the restrictions in the way we are supposed to think, and enter into the world of creative thoughts. They have fewer barriers to where their thoughts take them. From this, an ADHD child can be very creative and think of amazing ideas outside of the box. Maybe this is why Einstein, who likely had ADHD, was such an incredible and creative inventor. Einstein said intelligence is not about the information it's about imagination.

It's a good point, because when the child is engaged in an activity that is interesting and/or stimulating, they usually don't show any signs of ADHD. Even a hyperactive ADHD child may sit perfectly still during a movie they enjoy. But that same child might rotate in an upside-down position in their chair when you try to do math flashcards to help them study for a test.

A good gauge of whether or not a child has ADHD is to ask, "How do they do when the activity is boring or not as stimulating?" We all have problems with boring tasks, but people without ADHD can say to themselves, "This is boring, but I'll push through it and get it done," and end up completing the task. They can make themselves do it. In contrast, an ADHD child may have the same thoughts and good intentions of getting it done but have serious problems making or willing themselves to

finish the task.

ADHD kids will start thinking about something more interesting or what they would rather be doing when uninterested. This becomes a distraction and they end up forgetting or missing an important part of the current task they are doing, resulting in work that is incomplete or work that looks carelessly completed. Here are a few examples:

At home:

- They throw all their clothing in the drawer but don't fold their clothes first.

- They often forget to flush the toilet or put the lid down.

- They take out the trash but don't put a new trash bag in the trash can.

- They do the dishes but don't wipe the counters or start the dishwasher.

At school:

- They turn in their assignment but don't put their name on it.

- They bring their backpack home but forget

their assignment.

- They finish their homework but forget to turn it in.

Most missed steps are accidental, but they also may skip a task on purpose to get the job done faster. For example, a child asked to clean up a small milk spill on the floor may decide to quickly use his sock on his foot to soak it up. The task was completed without adding the 4 additional boring steps of (1) walking over to get a paper towel, (2) bringing it back to the spill, (3) bending down to clean it up, and (4) going back to the trash to throw the towel away. Using the sock saved time and allowed him to more quickly move on to what he would rather be doing.

ADHD kids have higher occurrences of learning difficulties. ADHD has nothing to do with how smart a person is, but it can affect their ability to learn new things. These learning challenges can be related to not being able to focus on what is being taught, or they can come from issues with processing information slowly, or issues with short-term memory. Kids with ADHD may also have associated learning disorders like

dyslexia or dysgraphia. If your child has ADHD, it is always important to rule out learning disabilities.

ADHD kids have problems filtering or regulating themselves socially, emotionally, and physically. Think of the front part of the brain as a coffee filter (remember, this front part of the brain is where the ADHD physically resides). The job of a coffee filter is to regulate or control what goes into the coffee pot. The filter allows water to go through, but not the grounds. The "filter" of an ADHD child isn't working as well as it should. Using this example with ADHD, a child who doesn't have a properly working "filter" in his mind will have more problems regulating what "comes out" through their behavior and emotions.

Let's look at a situation where an ADHD boy is being teased. Multiple ideas pop into his mind about how to react and handle this situation, and because the filter is not working as it should, an inappropriate response may come out, such as pushing or hitting another child. The ADHD child often gets frustrated by his impulsive actions and will make comments that show

their self-frustration like, "I can't help it... I don't know why I did that... It just happened so fast."

It's not just emotion or behavior that is affected, but kids with ADHD are often hyperactive. (As mentioned before, girls with ADHD tend to not be as hyperactive as boys with ADHD.) Because they are not filtering their emotions or behavior as well, they may annoy or bother others. A child with an active filter will say to themselves, "I need to sit still now," or "I need to let the other person talk now." But an ADHD child has problems controlling their hyperactivity and impulses. In a classroom setting, instead of waiting for their turn, they may just blurt out the answer without waiting to be called on. If they are told to sit still in a chair, they will fidget, tip, bounce, twist, and squirm. Interestingly, physical activity is more regulated when they are doing something they enjoy, like watching TV or playing video games.

When the filter isn't working as well, the teacher or parent often has to act as the filter for that child to help regulate them. The adults have to make comments like, "Stop doing that and start your work," or "I can't understand

you, slow down," or "Stop swinging from the curtains." This constant need to help regulate will cause frustration for those working with the child and the ADHD child themselves.

ADHD kids also tend to be hyper-talkers. They may have problems regulating how much and how fast they talk with seemingly no regard for interrupting others. And because their internal thoughts often travel faster than they can talk, what they say may only be part of their point, causing confused communication.

CHAPTER - 23
EXAMPLE GAMES FOR ADHD KIDS TO FIND THEIR GIFTS

Making learning fun was a key learning from our ADHD superstars. This was the deciding factor about whether they could focus on it or not. I've included two examples of fun learning games to engage and excite children with ADHD

"Cramming Game"

As we know, forcing consistent learning on someone with ADHD can create resistance. Some of my friends found that a cramming approach to school work worked better for them than consistent learning. If a cramming approach seems to work well for your child, then you might consider understanding what factors are at play. Let's break it down to discover what's at the heart of cramming, and decide

whether we can use it in our approach.

Essentially, a cramming approach to studying is a great deal of energy being expended in a short period of time, due to either fear of failure or an incentive to do well. There is a deadline that needs to be met, which creates a large amount of motivation and energy to learn. Cramming is also a novelty, and isn't happening consistently on a day to day basis.

I'm not suggesting that you use the "fear" motivation approach at all, which seems to be used very often in a disciplinary environment. The fun approach sounds much more in tune with what the superstars are advocating.

Using a "deadline and incentive" game, to recreate the influences that induce "cramming" for exams, has the potential to be wonderfully fun when applied creatively. This might sound complicated, but it's not. A very simple model of this is a straight-forward treasure hunt. Solving clues to find toys or chocolate eggs is exactly the kind of activity that uses this approach in a fun way. The toys and eggs are the incentives, the other children looking are the deadline, as well as competition.

Adapting a treasure hunt into a "cramming" game:

Use a clue-based treasure hunt, so that your child guesses where to hunt next.

At each spot on the treasure hunt, you hide a reward, and a sheet of paper, with a passage of text for them to study.

A reward could be a chocolate egg, a marble, a token (representing points), a grape, a coin (this could be a fun way to give them their pocket money), depending on the age of the child.

Give them 3 minutes to study a passage, and try to remember it all. Take the paper away and ask a question about what they read.

To get the next clue, they must answer correctly, if they get it wrong, they get another question.

If they get 3 questions wrong, they have 1 more minute to study the piece of paper.

If the child can't read, the game can be made much simpler, with easier questions.

Adding excitement:

Think like a computer game: Introduce

changing time limits for studying up on the facts, bonuses (e.g., for 3 correct questions in a row they get an extra marble or egg), forfeits and penalties (e.g., Every time they get a question wrong, they have to stand on one leg for 30 seconds. Or repeat a silly rhyme. Or eat a cold baked bean. Or be squirted with a water pistol...)

Mum or dad might even be competing for the marbles or chocolate eggs. (You might pretend that you want your child to get the questions wrong, in order to get your sticky hands on their treasure. So, ask them the hardest questions first, to try and trip them up. And tell them what you're doing, and that you want their treasure for yourself. Compete with them.)

Don't be afraid to do something outrageous with them. The point is to make the game engaging, fun and motivating. You might want to forget about the hierarchy and rules for a while. You might introduce a rule that if they get 5 questions wrong in a row, they lose half the chocolate eggs they've collected.

Keep the pay-offs something that's highly desirable. You could choose simple incentives

like the person with the most points or eggs at the end of the game chooses their favorite meal or a piggyback from mum or dad. Or slightly self-deprecating incentives, such as the winner of the game getting to squirt mum or dad with a water pistol, or throw a bucket of cold water over them (if you have more than one child playing, they're all going to enjoy watching that).

For older children, you could create a "town" or "world" in your house, garden, or street, with a corresponding map. This might include historical landmarks, works of art, geographic regions, planets of the solar system, or even just colors and shapes. The choices are endless. Make sure that the questions you ask as clues all link back to the subject they are learning about!

Cooling down

If you're worried about over-excitement, be prepared with a "cool down" activity at the end of the game, such as musical statues, a meditation exercise, or a video to watch, to start calming them down.

Consider filming the game, so that you can watch the video back together, giving them a chance cool down and also to shout out the answers to the questions. That way, your children get to repeat the questions and answers again in a fun way, and repetition is very important to learning.

Tips

You don't need to go to great lengths preparing for the game. Simply photocopying pages from a textbook for them to study and hiding them around the living room with a clue on the back would suffice.

Think about the rules and incentives in advance, and explain them at the beginning. This makes things fair. If you don't explain to them at the start that every time, they get a question wrong, you're going to eat one of their chocolate eggs, they may get a little upset when you do.

Keep the goals, subjects, and incentives in line with your child's current life and learning abilities. You might need to adapt the game to keep it fun. For example, one week, your child might be very excited to play for fidget

spinners, the next week, fidget spinners could be incredibly uncool and uninteresting.

Never make a child feel stupid for not knowing an answer to a question. You might ruin the game, and perhaps even put them off learning. If they keep getting the wrong questions to give, consider giving them longer to study the text next time. If it's too difficult, consider making the text simpler or easier to read. Try and foster a feeling of success and confidence. If your game involves you directly competing with them, you might choose to jokingly "celebrate" when they get a question wrong because you're more interested in winning their chocolate eggs or marbles than you are in helping them learn. This will show them that the pressure is really off them, and they can relax. Also, it shows them that it's really down to them to learn for themselves this time.

You can accumulate previously used fact sheets, and even make corresponding "question cards" over the course of a school year, so that by the end of the school year, you have an enormous pile of relevant questions to re-use. This uses repetition to your child's advantage, but you

might not get so many chocolate eggs for yourself.

For older children, call the game a "mission," challenge, or orienteering, something more adult than a treasure hunt.

You can easily use an egg timer from a board game to time the cramming periods.

The key here is fun, something they will want to play again. Get creative with your "cramming" games, forget that your mum or dad for a while, and enjoy yourself as well.

Entrepreneurial Game

There are hundreds of ways you can encourage an ADHD child to be inventive, creative and persuasive, which will all benefit their entrepreneurial abilities as adults.

A very easy entrepreneurial game, focusing on the art of persuasion, might be to give your child a simple item like a pair of socks, and ask them to tell you why you should buy it, listing all of the positive qualities. If they can make you agree to buy them, they get a reward of some kind.

To make it more of a two-way exchange or debate, you could ask them to try and convince you to exchange the socks in their hands, with the pair you are currently wearing. Why should you go to all of the effort to take off your socks for their pair? Make it harder for them by giving them an old pair with holes in them, or a big woolly pair even though it's the middle of summer. If it's too difficult for them, make sure that the pair they are holding are much nicer (and fresher?) than the pair you have on. You can help them if needed by hinting at the more obvious benefits to the exchange.

Tip

Don't expect a child to be a sales genius without some practice, perhaps make it relatively easy for your child to persuade you the first time you play this game. You can become more of a challenging customer over time.

See where you can take the game, perhaps you might get them to start haggling for increased pocket money if they promise to provide additional washing up services, or they get an extra snack if they can convince you of the nutritional benefits.

If their improved persuasive skills spill over into the rest of your relationship, consider whether this is good or bad for them, even if you don't want to spend more time discussing your reasoning for rules. Persuasive skills are important and seem to come naturally to some people with ADHD. Whilst this can be inconvenient for disciplinary figures like parents during childhood, persuasive skills as an adult are hugely important to success. Try not to squash them in an attempt to maintain control, as this can lead to frustration and rebellion. A suitable outlet such as a game like this, can help to develop persuasive skills, so that children don't think of them as inherently "wrong," whilst also giving them an arena.

CHAPTER - 24

ALTERNATIVE HEALTH & COMPLEMENTARY MEDICINE

More than 40% of all Americans use some form of complementary, alternative, or integrative medicine. While similar, each of these three (3) medical treatment types have a distinct meaning.

Complementary Medicine means using a non-mainstream medical approach in conjunction with conventional medicine, separating each into its own treatment. Alternative Medicine is when a non-mainstream medical approach is used in place or instead of a conventional approach. Integrative Medicine is combining a non-mainstream approach with conventional medicine to construct one unified treatment protocol.

Regardless of the exact approach, for our purposes, we will describe all three together under the term Alternative Medicine. To further

understand this non-mainstream medical approach, it worthwhile to note that most alternative therapies have two (2) first, is the use of all-natural products like herbs (botanicals), vitamins, and minerals and are collectively marketed as dietary supplements. In the past several years interest in dietary supplements has increased dramatically. The most popular supplements in recent years include fish oil and other omega 3s, Ginkgo Biloba, and echinacea. A second hallmark of most alternative medicine methods is the focus on mind and body practices. Common mind and body alternative therapies include acupuncture, massage therapy, movement therapies (like Pilates), meditation, and relaxation therapies accomplished through a breathing exercise, muscle relaxation, or guided imagery.

While alternative therapies were once dismissed by licensed physicians in recent years, it has rapidly received more acceptance in conventional Western medicine and has become increasingly commonplace for treatment of a large number of health conditions.

Nutrition

Doctors have long recognized the association between good nutrition and good health. Nutrition is the science of foods and nutrients contained in food. Nutrients found in food are used by the body to support growth, provide energy, and maintain and support body tissue. Thus, the study of nutrition examines the relationship between diet and health, including the relationship between diet and disease. Examples of chronic health conditions commonly associated with nutrition include Cardiovascular Disease, Obesity, Type II Diabetes, Osteoporosis, and Hypertension.

National Institutes of Health Office of Dietary Supplements (ODS)

The National Institutes of Health Office of Dietary Supplements (ODS) is an office of the National Institutes of Health and provides users a searchable database containing bibliographic information about nutrition and health and disease. The database called the International Bibliographic Information on Dietary Supplements, or IBIDS for short can be accessed free of charge.

The IBIDS database is provided under a collaborative effort between the National Institutes of Health and the U.S. Department of Agriculture. Searching the database simply involves typing your search terms in the box and selecting "Search."

Biotechnology & Patents

Biotechnology is the application of technology to manufacture products that improve biological processes for the benefit of living organisms. In medicine, biotechnology is the basis for the development of pharmaceutical drugs, diagnostic and testing equipment, surgical implants, assisted living devices, and nearly every other tangible product that improves patient lives and outcomes.

A patent is a form of intellectual property. Intellectual property is distinct from tangible property and refers to creations of the mind. Just as physical property rights protect a person from encroachment on tangle items, intellectual property rights protect a person from the encroachment of creations of the mind. Intellectual property is generally divided into two categories, industrial property, and

copyright. Most often, copyright applies to artistic works, like song lyrics, music scores, poems, novels, artistic paintings, photographs, and sculptures. Industrial property includes trademarks, industrial design, and patents and generally applies to physical items that are of utility for human use. Industrial property includes the ideas, thought, and the reason that form the basis of an invention and are commonly expressed in mathematical calculations, engineering design, and the manipulation and combination of chemical processes and properties.

Most biotechnological creations are protected by patents. Most often, intellectual property rights are asserted to prohibit another party from using creations of the mind in their own profit-making ventures. In addition to patents and copyright, two other common types of intellectual property are trademark and trade secrets. It is important to remember that intellectual property rights do not imply ownership, but rather the right to control the commercialization of the ideas or expression in question.

Patents can be an excellent source of information about not only patented drugs and medical devices but about disease and health conditions in general. Since patents are organized in a uniform and consistent manner, the introduction or background section can provide an excellent review of current scientific literature about the disease and also detailed discussions about various health care topics.

Since patent applications are filed as long as five years before patent approval, these filings can give the researcher a glimpse into the future of the treatment, and sometimes even cures for various diseases and health conditions.

While three types of patents can be granted, the two most common patents related to health care are Utility Patents and Design Patents. Utility patents protect inventions and discoveries of useful and new processes, machines, articles of manufacture, or "compositions of matter." As the name implies, design patents protect the drawings, charts, etc. that establish the shape and physical characteristics of an object to be manufactured. The third type of patent is the Plant Patent and is reserved for the discovery

or invention of a new variety of "asexually" reproduced plant. Again, plant patents are uncommon in biotechnology.

Clinical Guidelines

As the name implies, a clinical guideline is a document that outlines the clinical management of a disease or health condition. In this regard, a clinical guideline can be viewed as a blueprint for the doctor and health care team to follow to diagnosis, manage, and treat specific health conditions in patients. Like any blueprint, however, the doctor must also incorporate her knowledge, experience, and best professional judgment and alter her application of a clinical guideline by taking into consideration the particular physical and emotional state of the patient, as well as the patients set of values and beliefs. Therefore, in practice, the use of clinical guidelines by physicians is just that, a guideline used in conjunction with several other considerations to determine patient care.

Clinical guidelines generally cover every aspect of patient care, from diagnosis to treatment and prognosis and continuing care. The clinical

guideline will typically also outline the risks and benefits of a course of action, as well as cost-effectiveness.

An important societal objective of clinical guidelines is to standardize medical care, thereby allowing patients regardless of income or socioeconomic status to receive the same high-quality medical care.

Agency for Healthcare Research and Quality (AHRQ)

Clinical guidelines are generally collected and approved, and frequently written by a national health care agency. In the United States, the U.S. Agency for Healthcare Research and Quality (AHRQ) acts as the clearinghouse for clinical guidelines even though many are written by professional medical and doctor and associations. The AHRQ collection of guidelines which can be accessed at Searching clinical guidelines at AHRQ is easy as the site uses similar syntax as a normal web search. Thus, to find a guideline for treating a specific disease simply enter your term in the search box. Likewise, to search for guidelines for conditions containing multiple words or phrases, enclose

your terms in quotation marks. Finally, Boolean searches can be performed using "and" or "or" between words and concepts of interest.

Drugs & Medications

Drugs are chemical substances that have a biological effect on humans and animals. Drugs are used by physicians to treat, cure, prevent, and even diagnose disease. Additionally, drugs can be used to enhance or improve mental or physical or well-being. Both prescription and over-the-counter drugs play several important roles in medicine. Drugs used to prevent disease are known as Prophylactic Drugs, drugs used to relieve symptoms are called Palliative Drugs and drugs used to cure disease are Therapeutic Drugs. Drugs for these purposes are also called medications or medicine, thus distinguishing them from drugs used for recreational or illicit purposes.

While all approved drugs have specific medicinal properties, most also have side effects. Side effects are secondary effects of medication that generally have no therapeutic value in the cure, treatment, or prevention of disease. Side effects can be both good and bad but are most often the

latter. One major challenge drug manufacturers face developing medications that maximize the therapeutic effects of a drug while minimizing side effects. When prescribing medications or recommending over-the-counter alternatives, doctors consider both the "good" and the "bad" when determining the best course of medicinal treatment for patients.

Prescription and Over-the-Counter Drugs and Medications

The best single resource to research drugs and medications is the Drug Information Portal administered by the National Institutes of Health (NIH). Unlike a standard web database, a portal is a site that functions as a point of access to multiple search engines or databases on the Internet.

CONCLUSION

People who have children or who will be fathers and mothers have concerns and questions about how to raise them. They will also want to find out more about what kinds of things should and should not be done when building children of all ages. Raising the children is a good investment for anyone who wants to learn more about being a mom or dad, and you will get many benefits from using it.

Child development guidelines are the main subject of many child-raising guidelines. Emphasis is placed on proper development as it will determine how your children will grow and how well their smart and interpersonal skills will grow. For example, many scientific studies, as well as childcare books, say that children develop better and are more likely to be smarter if they are exposed to music and art early, even when they are in their mother's womb. The childcare book will discuss how you can educate boys and girls about art and music, what types of music will help growth

and learning, and other ingredients that have a positive impact on children's development.

Nutrition is another major theme of the parenting books, which affects children's physical and intellectual growth. Your children will need enough nutrients to maintain their bodies and to help them become healthier and better against viruses and diseases. Proper nutrition also affects psychological development because the right type of food will contribute to brain functioning. The childcare guide provides a list of nutritional ingredients of mom and dad suitable for children of all ages and with more minerals and vitamins. In addition, childcare books will address the types of food that should be restricted or kept away.

But if your child has ADHD or is unable to focus on it, this strategy will help parents to help their children become more successful in school, learn more and be more co-operative at home. Teachers' notes: some of these strategies will also work in your classroom. And you can certainly advise them to parents.

Remind him to remind him that he must stay in the office when he is working. This means that

it must focus on: thinking, reading, writing, and speaking.

ADHD medication. If various strategies fail, and your child has difficulty staying focused, your doctor can recommend treatment. With the right choice and dosage, the increase can be remarkable. But be sure to consult with a doctor who is familiar with ADHD stimulant drugs. Most pediatricians do not get much training in neuropsychopharmacology. Ask for a referral to a child psychiatrist. You want to make sure your child gets the best medicine and the right amount.

ADHD diet. Sometimes food affects children in unexpected ways. If you think that diet may be a problem, consult your doctor. Make sure your child eats healthy food. Many foods can contain sugar, processed protein, and are inadequate to make your baby act the way you think he might have ADHD. You have to have a healthy breakfast.

Now choose one of these strategies at once. And because parents are good to introduce to children, let your child choose the one they like best. Add other activities to the list in

stages. You will soon discover what works and doesn't work. Teacher, you can choose one or two strategies that will work in school to help children with ADHD in your class.

In most cases, children will ask their own questions and do it last time. Stubbornness is a good example of unfavorable behavior in the usual background of any age group. Childcare guidelines will provide you with verification techniques to defeat insults and reduce those behaviors.

However, there are a number of serious features and trends that need to be addressed as soon as possible, and fathers and mothers must use age-appropriate techniques for their children. Independence, intimidation, attacks, and insults are certainly not recommended; Child coaching guidelines will tell you how you can avoid dangerous situations like this, plus how you can handle them if they arise.

Of course, child coaching books look at extraordinary behavior and how to get to know your girls and boys if they respect your rules and do what they have to do. Responsibility is a kind of positive behavior that all children

and mothers of their children want to have and express. Suggest that child development guides usually do what fathers and mothers need to learn how to be responsible, especially when they are around their children. This will allow their sons and daughters to know and say it, even when they are adults. Make sure boys and girls build themselves up, do homework from time to time, clean the bedroom, and take care of pets as actions that will advance responsibility.

Self-esteem is a feature of everybody, and it is important that children develop self-esteem early on. Confidence and a sense of identity will help them when they start school and connect with other girls and boys. In addition, girls and boys were found to be happier, more social, and often successful in everyday life.

Simply put, the parenting guide is designed to help you find out about parenting, how to prepare for it, and what you would expect from the most demanding job in your life.

My thanks go to all of you, readers, I thank you for travelling with me through the complicated world of ADHD. I am glad to have shared with

you the effective advices and the best strategies I still adopt for the growth of my children.

With practice and persistence, parenting an ADHD child will get better. Remember your child's behavior isn't a reflection of your parenting ability, so don't be discouraged. With this in mind, change your parenting style to help your child deal with his impulsiveness, inattentiveness, and defiance.

Be kind to your child, but also to yourselves.

Good luck!

Printed in Great Britain
by Amazon

51708478R00174